Feminism in Modern English Drama

Feminism in Modern English Drama (1892-1914)

Swapan Kumar Banerjee

ATLANTIC

PUBLISHERS & DISTRIBUTORS (P) LTD

Published by

ATLANTIC

PUBLISHERS & DISTRIBUTORS (P) LTD

7/22, Ansari Road, Darya Ganj,
New Delhi-110002
Phones : +91-11-40775252, 23273880, 23275880, 23280451
Fax : +91-11-23285873
Web : www.atlanticbooks.com
E-mail : orders@atlanticbooks.com

Branch Office
5, Nallathambi Street, Wallajah Road,
Chennai-600002
Phones : +91-44-64611085, 32413319
E-mail : chennai@atlanticbooks.com

Printed in India at Nice Printing Press, A-33/3A, Site-IV,
Industrial Area, Sahibabad, Ghaziabad, U.P.

Dedicated to the memory of

Mother Teresa (1910-1997)

who showed us what a woman can do.

PREFACE

I firmly believe that those who are interested in English plays have great admiration for Bernard Shaw. Highly impressed by his female protagonists, I have attempted to see his women characters from a different perspective in the present book. I have also explored the plays of Granville Barker and John Galsworthy and hold the view that the New Woman was not a unique invention of Shaw, but a new wave which swept the contemporary society.

In the history of English plays, however, the publication of Shaw's *Widowers' Houses* marks the emergence of the New Woman—a new class that was educated, daring and assertive. The New Women found significant place even in the major plays of Shaw's contemporaries, Barker and Galsworthy. They were no longer mere dutiful daughters, rather they set a new trend by challenging male authority and attempting to remake the world created by men. They are, in fact, the precursor of the modern heroine with autonomy and equal rights. Accordingly, they deserve a detailed study, and the present book *Feminism in Modern English Drama* is one such attempt.

The present book explores the nature and role of the New Woman in its entirety. It critically examines the early and middle plays of Shaw, from *Widowers' Houses* to *Pygmalion,* and attempts to trace the impact of the contemporary wave of feminism on Galsworthy's plays and letters. Galsworthy's concern for women has often been overlooked in critical studies. The book also offers an in-depth study of Barker's New Woman as moral genius. Needless to mention, the book will prove highly useful to the students of English literature of all levels. For me, it is a pleasure that many readers can now share the fruits of my toil and avail of the guidance to carry on further research work in related fields.

I have been fortunate to receive encouragement, guidance and cooperation from many people in accomplishing this great task. I take this opportunity to express my gratitude to all who contributed to the making of this book. I must make a particular reference to Prof. Mihir Ranjan Bhattacharya of English Department, Jadavpur University, who encouraged me to express my thoughts and ideas in the present form. I am sincerely thankful to him. Special thanks are to Dr. Visvanath Chatterjee, former Head, Department of English, Jadavpur University, and Dr. Sajni Mukherjee, an Oxford scholar and former Head, Department of English, J.U., for their inspiration and cooperation.

Finally, I owe my thanks to Dr. K.R. Gupta, Chairman, Atlantic Publishers and Distributors, for this eloquent production.

SWAPAN KUMAR BANERJEE

CONTENTS

INTRODUCTION 1

The dramatic revival of the late Victorian and Edwardian era (1892-1913) was rich in revolutionary ideas. A new theatrical renaissance was ushered in with the publication of Bernard Shaw's *Widowers' Houses* (1892) under the combined influences of the Norwegian dramatist Henrik Ibsen on the one hand, and the economic outlook of Karl Marx on the other. The intellectual drama of Shaw and his contemporaries, Harley Granville Barker and John Galsworthy, used the theatre as a social force by raising questions as to the sanity of the existing social systems and structures. Technically the 'new drama' broke away from the conventions of the well-made plays. Another noteworthy feature was the emergence of the New Woman, a new breed that was educated, bold and assertive. For the first time significant stage roles were created for women and women's questions got the importance they deserved. The New Women were inducted into the early and middle plays of Shaw, the major plays of Granville Barker and the late plays of Galsworthy. They eschewed their traditional roles of dutiful daughters and submissive wives and seized the role of the protagonist. They set a new trend by challenging male authority and attempting to remake the world created by men.

A study of the role of the New Woman in the late Victorian novels of George Eliot, Meredith, Moore, Gissing and Hardy was carried out by Lloyd Fernando.[1] In another study of similar nature entitled *Women and Fiction: Feminism and the Novel* (1880-1920) Patricia Stubbs pointed out how the mid-Victorian novelists uncritically reflected the dominant assumptions of their time.[2] The winds of change were brought about by the late nineteenth century writers with their keen sense of realism. Though in the novels of H.G. Wells economic independence of women was emphasized, feminism ran a poor second best to eugenics and the welfare of the state.[3] In contrast to the treatment of women by Wells and Lawrence as sexual and impulsive partners, Virginia Woolf concentrated on the everyday reality of their lives and protested against the falsification of women's nature.[4] The 'new drama' came to be noted for their revolutionary ideas and a new mind-set. But the emergence of the New Woman and her contribution to modern drama has not received much serious attention in the volumes of critical studies of the two major critical works on Shavian women, Barbara B. Waston's *A Shavian Guide to Intelligent Women*, a general study of various types of women having the common traits of 'wit and will'. While appreciating the individuality of the Shavian woman as a triumphant feature, she does not venture into the plays of Shaw's contemporaries for similar traits. Another important critical study—*The Unwomanly Woman in Bernard Shaw's Drama* (1973) by Sonja Lorichs also treats the New Woman as an isolated phenomenon, exclusively Shavian. She has selected only six plays *Mrs. Warren's Profession*, *Major Barbara*, *Getting Married*, *Fanny's First Play*, *Pygmalion*, and *Saint Joan*, to present the characteristic traits of these new heroines in English drama.[5] But the significant role played by the New Woman in shaping the course of modern drama remains unrecognized. *Fabian Feminist: Bernard Shaw and Woman* (1977) edited by Rodelle Weintraub attempts to explore the political, economic, mythic or literary factors that influenced such female characterization and to furnish new insights into his work and into women. The editor in her introduction has highlighted the eternal freshness of Shavian ideas and discovered much affinity between Fabian feminism and the goals of contemporary feminism. She criticizes Shakespeare for bowing down to male chauvinism in *The Taming of the Shrew* and compliments Shaw for substituting conventional morality with his original view of morality. However, in the same book Elsie Adams has discredited Shaw by arguing that more often than not he creates women characters who belong to types familiar in western literature.[6]

The theoretical approach I have applied can neither be strictly called feminist criticism nor can it be justly called psycho-analytic interpretation; but their combined influence has helped me to explore the nature and role of the New Woman. No pretension of exploring the nature of the female world is made; it has been successfully done by distinguished feminists like Simone de Beauvoir and Virginia Woolf. Though the word 'sexuality' has multiple meanings, I have used it to mean gender identity or gendered subjectivity: a sense of ourselves as masculine or feminine. Distinction is made in modern feminism between sex and gender: the former is a matter of biology while the latter is a social construct—something learnt or acquired rather than naturally inherited. It is best summed up by Simone de Beauvoir: 'One is not born, but rather becomes, a woman.[7]

Much of Lacan's abstract and abstruse theory has little relevance to the New Woman's impact on modern drama. He rejects conventional characterization in literature on the ground that the self is not a real entity—a mere linguistic assemblage of the signifiers clustering round a proper name. This rejection of self as a unique, separate entity leads to repudiation of literary realism. So far as women's 'social castration' and 'penis envy' are concerned, they have been best countered by Simone de Beauvoir who argued that lack of phallus has been duly compensated by the exclusive reproductive capacity of women.[8] But with Shaw, Lacan would have agreed that women's subservient status in patriarchal culture is an undeniable fact. The glory of men's success is built on the denigration of women. The New Woman's endeavour is a struggle to become a subject from the traditional role of an object.

The object of my study is to fill the gap in criticism by closely examining the nature and role of the New Woman and tracing her emergence as a product of the time—a social phenomenon rather than a Shavian innovation. I have examined the early and middle plays of Shaw, from *Widowers' Houses* (1892) to *Pygmalion* (1914) and referred to relevant letters and Prefaces. As Granville Barker revised his plays several times and texts of different editions are available, I have consulted Dennis Kennedy's Cambridge edition of his plays (1987) and the revised version of *The Madras House* (1925). His letters to Shaw, which could have been vital primary documents, have been unfortunately destroyed. Galsworthy's plays and letters have been studied to prove that even a conservative dramatist like him could not remain unaffected by the contemporary wave of feminism. The weak women of his early plays, the 'Womanly Women' are substituted by strong and independent women in *The Eldest Son* and *The Fugitive*. Relevant biographical discussions of the playwrights seem unavoidable in the assessment of the impact of real women on the dramatists as well as on their creations. The novels of the two major dramatists have some relevance to my study. Though Shaw's novels were unsuccessful and unread, they have academic interest. His New Women appeared in the novels much earlier than his plays. Similarly, a brief discussion of the heroine of *The Forsyte Saga* has become pertinent, though the novels are literary production of a much later period.

The social, political and economic backgrounds have been duly considered. Ibsen has been discussed as the literary precursor and the mainspring of inspiration. The emphasis has been on the contribution of the New Woman to women's causes and the new vistas opened and dimensions added to drama. As a visionary Shaw not only reflected the first phase of the feminist struggle (e.g. the suffragette movement) but also anticipated vital questions regarding woman's position raised by the women's liberation movement of the 1960's and 1970's. The 'Unwomanly Women' of Shavian plays are angry women who set out to correct the male-dominated culture by sheer force of personality and indomitable will. The conflict between good and evil of the conventional drama is substituted by the battle of sexes in which more often than not women triumph; from a position of passive suffering and sacrifice, women emerge as decision-makers. This trend continues in the major plays of Granville Barker. As a versatile director, actor, playwright and scholar who staged major Shavian plays, he also was occupied with the crucial problems of his age:

'women' and 'money'. If Shavian women are called 'vital geniuses' for their unusual enterprise and energy, Granville Barker's women deserve to be called 'moral geniuses' for their extraordinary courage and integrity of character. They wage a fierce battle against corrupt men in power and often meet with tragic consequences. It is unfortunate that in spite of the efforts of Margery Morgan and Eric Salmon to arouse interest in Granville Barker the dramatist, neither his plays nor his women characters have received serious attention.

After his early success with conventional plays Galsworthy responded to 'the microbe of freedom ... in the air'.[9] His personal life as well his literary career was influenced by a New Woman, Ada Galsworthy (née Cooper). The women of his middle and late plays break away from Victorian stereotypes. They embraced hardship in following their conscience often in defiance of the dictates of male society. While Galsworthy the writer of problem plays is well known, his concern for women has been overlooked in critical studies. I have confined my study to the plays of Shaw, Granville Barker and Galsworthy which were either published or performed between 1892 and 1914. Occasional references have been made to some thematically related plays beyond this period. The plays of Synge and Yeats have been deliberately excluded because of their preoccupation with the poetically rich life of Ireland with its genial humour and their rejection of the joyless and pallid naturalism of Ibsen and his followers.

Though the New Women do not profess to be feminists, they show deep concern for women's status in society. They aim at transformation of society by changing people's perception to the issues. I have used the term 'new woman' to include all spirited women in the plays under review. The phrase was coined by Sarah Grand in *The American Review* in 1894: 'The New Woman became many things to many people, but for all she stood bold, free and capable of thinking and acting for herself. The retiring dimpled virgin, decorative and obedient, was brushed aside by the modern girl who read, knew and understood and refused to sit quietly in a corner.[10] The New Woman of the nineteenth century is the precursor of the modern heroine with autonomy and equal rights. She is a threat to the male ego so long accustomed to occupying centre stage. A shift in gender bias is noticeable: women become the subject of drama and mistresses of their own destinies. Shaw's attempt to create the Superman was a fiasco, but his New Woman was closer to Superwoman. She ushered in a new power equation and improved the quality of drama.

I have deliberately avoided interchanging 'New Woman' with 'feminist'; the subtle difference is best highlighted again by Sarah Grand in *The New Aspect of the Woman's Question*. Never tired of reiterating that woman was never meant to be a developed man, she defined a New Woman thus:

> 'One who, while retaining all the grace of manner and feminine charm, had thrown off all the silliness and hysterial feebleness of her sex and improved herself so as to be in everyway the best companion for man and without him the best fitted for a place of usefulness in the world.'[11]

Though not overtly feminist, a great deal of modern feminism is surprisingly anticipated in the plays under review. The New Woman has her literary as well as social counterparts. Ibsen's Nora came to be associated with the assertion of women's rights, but it was Lona Hessel who first emerged as the New Woman in *The Pillars of Society* (1877). The heroines of *The Lady from the Sea* and *Rosmersholm* are surprisingly the prototypes of modern independent women of the twentieth century. The real life counterparts were Mrs. Emmeline Pankhurst, Lydia Becker, Annie Besant and Beatrice Webb who launched various liberation movements to extricate women from systematic exploitation. The literary characters shared their vitality and reforming zeal and worked for a better world of equal rights and opportunities.

As a distinct theatrical genre feminist theatre (viz. the plays of Caryl Churchill, Pam Gems et al) emerged in 1960s in Britain and U.S.A., but its foundation was laid by Shaw and his contemporaries. The focus on the condition of women as women was a new consciousness which brought a new vitality to the 'new' drama. The women characters are seen struggling to free themselves from the male domination often with success. They ask subversive questions, often come up with new ideas and set out to implement them with gusto. This new breed of intellectual women is unknown in Shakespeare. They also fare better than the rebellious heroines of Pinero and Jones who are punished with death for transgressing the moral codes of Victorian society. The dramatists have emphasized their personalities and their social importance by underplaying their sexual role and feminine charm.

Like Freud and Lacan, Shaw regarded sexual identity as a cultural construct and opposed 'essentialism' which presupposes some natural essence of the feminine that is universal and unchangeable. It is no mean achievement for Shaw to anticipate a century earlier, anti-essentialism which is a dominant critical theory of the mid 1990s. Freud is criticized by the feminist for his negative view of woman's sexuality which is based on feelings of narcissism, masochism and her inherent inferiority complex known as 'penis envy'. Jacques Lacan who emphasized the unconscious as the nucleus of our being and the inadequacy of the existing language for women was enthusiastically received by French feminists like Helen Cixous and Julia Kristeva. Like Virginia Woolf he admitted that language is biased in favour of the male and a new language needs to be invented to represent their repressed feelings and emotions. But like Shaw, Lacan never came to realise that natural feminine behaviour is nothing but the acting out of the requirement of a patriarchal society. Another French thinker who deserves mention in any discussion of women's emancipation is Michel Foucault. He challenged the Freudian and Marxist interpretation of sexuality and analysed the impact of discourses on sexuality on western culture. The pseudo sexual liberation of women, he argues, is only a camouflaged bondage. Like Shaw he believes that only desexualisation of women can advance their causes. He is concerned with sexuality as a manifestation of social control and power over life. The New Woman's struggle also aims at counteracting the male domination or phallocentrism of the Victorian era. In a study devoted to ascertain the change in the existing power structure references to Lacan and Foucault are unavoidable. Shaw was the first British dramatist to realize how deep-seated women's bondage was. In a speech delivered at King's Theatre on 20th May, 1927 he admonished the British public for 'the extraordinary neglect of women's causes'. Victorian women underestimated themselves and glorified their menfolk who in their turn would put them on pedestal as angels. Men never bothered to understand them as they really are. Even three decades after the Victorian era Shaw noted that this attitude persisted. He asserted:

> 'I am telling you all this with a serious purpose. The dress has changed, the morality has not. People are still full of the old idea that woman is a special creation. I am bound to say that of late years she has been working extremely hard to eradicate that impression, and make one understand that a woman is really only a man in petticoats, or, if you like, that a man is a woman without petticoats.'[12]

Shaw went further to explain the secret of his success with women characters. 'I have always assumed', he added, 'that a woman is a person like myself, that is how the trick is done.'[13] The desexualisation of the heroine is a great achievement of Shaw. The Shavian insight is, interestingly enough, supported by the result of modern scientific research. J. Bronowski pointed out that sexual morphism is minimum in the human species. In the biological as well as cultural sense there is much less difference between men and women than there is in other species. Bronowski interpreted this general equality as an important achievement in the evolution of man.[14] An attack on androgyny came from a recent study named *Men are from Mars, Women are from Venus* by John Gray, M.D. His contention that men are unable to communicate effectively because of their gender and hormonal differences. But this fallacy is refuted by Brant Burleson, Professor of Communication at Purdue University, who maintained that men are not as gifted as women at some style of communication, not because of their sexual difference but because they have not been taught the skills.

Simone de Beauvior perceived a striking similarity between the bondage of woman 'truly feminine—that is frivolous, infantile, irresponsible' and the Negro 'with his dormant, childish, merry soul' as both were held back by a repressive master class.[15] She appreciated the Shavian polemics about the mechanism of oppression of the exploited classes. According to Shaw, the American whites relegated the Black to the rank of shoeshine boy and concluded that the Black was good for nothing but shining shoes. The vicious circle of inferiority was thus perpetuated.

The New Woman in the plays under review brings with her a new morality which clashes with the old morality. The conventional dramatic conflict between the hero and the stereotype villain is often superseded by a power struggle between the sexes. Shaw deals with it overtly in discussion while Galsworthy and Granville Barker employ the subtle technique of action and suggestion to achieve the same goal.

Though women are universally known for their better language skill, Victorian women spent their life in studied silence—a virtue extolled by the dominant group. Elizabeth Barrett Browning satirized the model woman in her long feminist poem, *Aurora Leigh*. In an age when women enjoyed little freedom of speech, the Shavian woman breaks this imposed silence with a vengeance. She is often more articulate in expressing her views than her male counterpart. The polemics of the New Woman is a feature that distinguishes her from her predecessors in the theatre. The range of topics discussed and debated is surprisingly wide: from politics to philosophy and from eugenics to human psychology.

The New Woman had the task of battling against age-old customs, traditions and superstitions. According to Aristotle, the female is distinguished by virtue of a certain lack of qualities and female nature is always afflicted with an inherent defectiveness. St. Thomas for his part defined woman as an imperfect man. Even today 'man' designates human beings in general while 'woman' represents the negative aspects of humanity. Her body is still regarded as a hindrance, a prison weighed down by numerous limitations. Shaw and his colleagues believed that the liberation of woman was closely tied up with other social issues; so, without restructuring society and changing its goals, women's status would not improve permanently.

It is admitted that women's problems as seen by the male dramatists suffer from certain limitations and can never match the feminine insight of Simone de Beauvoir and Virginia Woolf. This difference in perception is an unalterable fact which simply cannot be wished away. In her political autobiography, *The Downing Street Years*, Margaret Thatcher with her no-nonsense attitude made it clear when she was asked how she felt as a woman Prime Minister. She pointed out the futility of the question as she never experienced the other alternative.[16] Simone de Beauvoir also wrote that there will always be certain differences between man and woman; her eroticism and therefore her sexual world, have a special form of their own and therefore cannot fail to engender a sensuality, a sensitivity of a special nature.[17] This sexual difference, I believe, in no way undermines the achievements of the male dramatists. The New Woman's emergence in the dramatic revival brought a new power equation in the theatre. The monopoly of the central figure by male characters gives way to the assertive heroine. Thus an understanding of the role of the New Woman is central to the appreciation of modern drama. Her induction by Shaw is a turning point; and since then the assertive and independent heroine has become a permanent feature of modern drama.

NOTES AND REFERENCES

1. Lloyd Fernando, *New Woman in the Late Victorian Novel* (London, Pennsylvania Un. 1977).
2. Patricia Stubbs, *Women and Fiction: Feminism and the Novel* (London Methuen, 1979), p. 32.
3. *Women and Fiction*, p. 189.
4. *Women and Fiction*, p. 229.
5. Sonja Lorichs, *The Unwomanly Woman in Bernard Shaw's Drama* (Uppasala, Uppasala Un., 1973), p. 14.

6. Rodelle Weintraub, ed., *Fabian Feminist: Bernard Shaw and Woman* (University Park, Pennsylvania Un., 1977), p. 156.
7. Simone de Beauvoir, *The Second Sex*, trsl. & ed., H.M. Parshley (London, Four Square Books, 1960), p. 8.
8. *The Second Sex*, p. 411.
9. John Galsworthy, *A Family Man*, (London, Duckworth, 1992), p. 67.
10. Quoted in Kersley Gillian's *Darling Madame* (London, Virago, 1983), p. 77.
11. *Ibid.*
12. Bernard Shaw, *Platform and Pulpit*, ed., Dan H. Laurence (London, Rupert Hart Davis, 1962), p. 174.
13. *Ibid.*
14. J. Bronowski, *The Ascent of Man* (London, B.B.C., 1990), pp. 400-401.
15. Simone de Beauvoir, *The Second Sex*, trsl. & ed., H.M. Parshley (London, 1953), p. 310.
16. The *Downing Street Years* (London, Harper Collins, 1993), p.18.
17. Simone de Beauvoir, *The Second Sex*, trsl, & ed., H.M. Parshley (London, Four square Books, 1960), p. 415.

THE SETTING AND SCENARIO

2

I

The emergence of the New Woman in late nineteenth century Britain was not an isolated phenomenon: various social, political and educational reforms were responsible for her appearance. This chapter explores these factors as well as the impact of the new literary model of heroine introduced by Ibsen. Contemporary Victorian women who dedicated themselves to the task of raising women's status have been briefly delineated to show how the stage characters were influenced by real women. Many problems of women may be traced back to the economic problems of mid-nineteenth century England. As a result of industrialization the wealth and property of the country were unevenly distributed between the rich and the poor leading to growing discontent and class tension. A vast majority of common people were forced to live in abject poverty, squalor and frequent unemployment. The greater part of the nation's wealth was concentrated in the hands of a small minority of land and industry owners. Thus glaring contrast made the social reformers and political thinkers question the basic social structure.

In 1801 England and Wales had a population of nine million; a century later it increased to forty-one and half million. The reasons for this rapid growth in population were a decrease in death rate due to improved medical care and personal hygiene and absence of birth control. Infant mortality was reduced and life expectation for adults increased. This excess of births over deaths and lack of family planning were responsible for a sharp increase in the population.

A large population lived in urban industrial areas and worked in factories and offices. But their livelihood was subject to the alternating slump and boom caused by industrial competitors like Germany and U.S.A. The 3% unemployed workforce of 1888 rose to 10% by 1886. In the wealthiest nation in the world, almost every twentieth inhabitant was a pauper; according to Poor Law reports, one-fifth of the community was insufficiently clad; according to medical reports to the Privy Council the agricultural labourers and large classes of working people in towns were too poorly fed to save them from what are known as starvation diseases. One third, if not indeed one half, of the families of the country are huddled, six in a room. In Germany of 1890s only 12.8% women had a recognized occupation. In Britain of 1911 only 10% had one.

The Poor Law was enacted to remedy these sufferings and hardships. Government tried to abolish pauperism as too many desperate paupers were a threat to the stability in society. Old Poor Laws made local magistrates responsible for providing help to paupers through unpaid overseers. Sometimes they were sent to the workhouse to provide them with work and discourage indolence. In the roundsman system paupers were sent round local employers to work for a fractional wage. Often the workhouse was a scene of filth, misery and diseases. The Speenhamland system took into account the price of bread and family size to determine the allowance. It encouraged growing population, low wages and demoralized the pauper. In 1832 the government set up a Royal Commission to investigate the Poor Law. The Report of Royal Commission held that the Speenhamland System was not only expensive but it also made poverty worse. As a result the Poor Law Amendment Act of 1834 came into effect. It was a centrally controlled system with its base in London. Under the new system workhouses were relatively cleaner and well-ordered but more strict than factories. Work was compulsory, punishment for misconduct harsh. Diets were wholesome but not palatable, unemployed husbands and wives were kept separately to prevent the birth of pauper children. After 1834 the cost of poor relief fell as the poor came to look upon the workhouse as an unattractive alternative. The workhouse or Poor Law relief was the only recourse for women with children when their husbands deserted them or squandered their wages. A report in 1909 found a 33% increase in the desertion of wives. They could sue for maintenance but a loophole in the law allowed them to avoid payment when in jail—an option often pursued.

The growing discontent among the poor and the threat of socialism emphasized the need for further reform. Between 1886 and 1903 Charles Booth carried on a private investigation of conditions relating to poverty in London. His *Life and Labour of the People of London* threw light on the causes of poverty and the factors that influenced the lives of the poor. Booth fixed the poverty line at about £1 a week and found that one third of the population fell below this line. He divided the population into eight classes and concluded that this great mass of poverty could not be solved by Poor Law or private charity: the state must intervene to ensure a minimum subsistence for the depressed 30% and provide old-age pension for elderly citizens. A few years later Seebohm Rowntree confirmed Booth's findings and highlighted how poverty affected the physical standards of children belonging to this 'have-not' group.

Working conditions in nineteenth century factories were harsh and unhealthy. The factories were overcrowded, and had poor ventilation and dangerous machinery. Harsh discipline including fines as punishment was imposed on workers. Children were employed to do dirty jobs for long hours at one third of an adult's wage. Shaw explored the mechanism of women's bondage and aimed at the total overhaul of the system. He deplored women's exploitation in the labour market in *The Intelligent Woman's Guide to Socialism and Capitalism*. He declared that under the Capitalist system women found themselves worse off than men because, as Capitalism made a slave of the man, and then, by paying the woman through him, made her his slave, she became the slave of a slave, which is the worst sort of slavery.[1] In 1840 the government set up a Royal Commission of Inquiry into Children's Employment in mines and factories. The Report published in 1842, exposed horrifying facts such as women engaged in hauling coal in mines with belts around their waist and chains passing between their legs like animals. Eight-year-old children worked as 'trappers' operating the ventilation door in the shafts and passed their time in isolation and darkness. At Hopwood's pit at Barnsley, the boys and girls worked naked to the waist.

G.M. Young gives us a moving description of a factory worker's life in his *Victorian England: Portrait of an Age*.

> 'The life within the factory or the mine was doubtless rigorous, and to children often cruel, but the human frame is immensely resilient and with such care as many employers took, the working hours of a labour's life were his happiest, but the imagination can hardly apprehend the horror in which thousands of families a hundred years ago were born, dragged out ghastly lives and died: the drinking water brown with faecal particles, the corpses kept unburied for a fortnight in a festering London August; mortified limbs quivering with maggots; and sleeping-dens afloat with sewage.'[2]

Working people began their campaign for a better Parliament that would look after their needs. In 1836 they placed what came to be known as the People's Charter with six demands such as vote for Member of Parliament, their payment, equal constituencies and Annual Parliament, vote by ballot, and abolition of property criterion for a voter. Their demands were strongly opposed by the upper and middle classes and were rejected. But gradually these demands were accepted into law. Various laws passed after 1850 concentrated on the protection of workers from unfair exploitation and health hazards. The Factories and Workshop Act of 1874 achieved the 10-hour day for all factory workers with a maximum limit of 56 hours of work per week.

By the turn of the century many laws were passed in favour of the working people. The Workmen's compensation Act of 1906 allowed workers earning less than £250 per annum to claim 50% of their wages if they lost their job owing to illness or injury. The National Insurance Act of 1911 ensured 7 shilling per week if workers become unemployed.

Another attempt to improve the condition of workers was the Trade Boards Act of 1909 which safeguarded the minimum wages of those who worked in small textile factories. The Coal Mines Act of 1911 banned employment of boys under 14 for underground work and required the levels of dust to be kept down to a minimum. The shop Act of 1912 guaranteed workers in retail trade a fixed lunch hour and a half day holiday. The old Age Pension Act of 1908 gave a pension of one to five shilling per week to people over 70. Shaw was acutely aware of the demoralizing effects of low wages of women and commented in *The Intelligent Women's Guide*: 'It is easy to ask a women to be virtuous; but it is not reasonable, if the penalty of virtue be starvation, and the reward of vice is immediate relief. If you offer a pretty girl two pence half-penny an hour in a match factory, with a chance of contracting necrosis of the jawbone from phosphorus poisoning on the one hand and on the other a jolly pampered time under the protection of a wealthy bachelor which was what the Victorian employers did and what employers still do all over the world...'[3]

In Victorian as well as Edwardian England life was indeed hard for woman. From their very childhood girls in middle class families were conditioned to believe that they had no duty beyond their family. The working girls had to do household chores after a day's hard work in factories. The family was dominated by the father who provided the income. This spirit of unchallenged male authority is faithfully reflected in contemporary drama. In St. John Ervine's *Progress* the prevailing notion of women's inferiority is mouthed by the distinguished scientist. He accused women for their lack of 'concentration' and 'complete impersonal devotion.'[4] Ironically the disparaging remark was hurled even after Marie Curie shared the Nobel Prize in 1903 with two other Physicist. A sardonic but fitting reply came from Virginia Wolf: 'Women have served all these centuries as looking glasses possessing the magic and delicious power of reflecting the figure of man at twice its natural size.'[5] The figures of Messeurs Voyshey and Madras loom large in Granville Barker's *The Voyshey*

Inheritances (1905) and *The Madras House*. Galsworthy's early plays like *The Silver Box* and *Strife* are dominated by imposing patriarchs. Similarly in Shaw's *Widowers' Houses* and *Major Barbara* we have two patriarchal families—a faithful portrayal of typical Victorian culture.

Young women's choice in the matter of marriage was very much restricted for economic reason: they had little opportunity to marry beyond their class. They had to marry the men they could get; and more often than not, they turned out to be the men they did not like. The fate of a few morganatics was unenviable. This class conflict is best expressed in Galsworthy's plays. The upper class women whiled away their time in playing tennis, golf, visiting friends and relatives, or reading fiction. Every family was fairly large. The mother was burdened with the onerous task of bringing up too many children which often jeopardized her health. The Church disapproved of birth control or abortion in the case of unwanted pregnancy. As a result women remain tied to their household chores and the upbringing of a large number of children.

In 1871 Annie Besant and Charles Bradlaugh were prosecuted for publishing pamphlets about countraception. From early life Annie Besant came to be distinguished as a social reformer and a Fabian Socialist. She worked with Shaw and had considerable influence on him. She served as a model for Raina in *Arms and the Man*. She helped Charles in his battle for a seat in the House of Commons against the law forbidding atheists from doing so. She also incurred the wrath of the government for her attempt to teach birth control publicly. The campaign for family planning bore fruit. In 1867 the birth rate in Britain was 36 per 1000 of population; in 1901 it fell to 28.6 per thousand; in 1905 it was further reduced to 27.2 per thousand.

In mid-nineteenth century England higher education and careers were considered unsuitable for women. The only respectable occupation open to them was the ill-paid job of governess. Even at the turn of the century their fate did not improve much. They worked as sales girls in the shops, did routine jobs at the post-office, and at best served as school mistresses. Women could study medicine and law but were discriminated against for practising as doctors or barristers. The women's colleges at Oxford and Cambridge allowed the girls to take examinations but they were debarred from receiving the degrees. It was only in 1878 that London University started to confer degrees on women. In Shaw's *Mrs. Warren's Profession* Vivie Warren qualifies herself as a professional actuary. But a large number of women belonging to all sections lived in colossal ignorance. It was argued that education of girls damaged their health, fertility and attractiveness to suitors. Sports for women were also discouraged on the same ground. Mr. Marriot Watson argued that the increasing participation of women in play or exercise would only create gaunt, flat-chested women prone to illness and infertility. Another limiting factor for women was their dress. The heavy clothes and corsets prevented them from moving freely, and taking part in sports and outdoor activities. The signs of emancipation were by and large confined to middle-class women. Sex without marriage and adultery were, however, common in aristocratic and fashionable circles in large cities.

In a society which preached puritanism and practised secret immorality, women become easy targets for public scandal. Publicity of any immoral conduct on the part of a women, whether married or not, meant loss of reputation which often forced her to a life of prostitution and penury. A social scandal sometimes proved so deadly that the victim committed suicide. But the men could survive these without either losing social position or power. This impelled Shaw to a further tirade against Capitalism: 'In short Capitalism acts on women as a continual bribe to enter into sex relations for money, whether in or out of marriage; and against this bribe there stands nothing beyond the traditional respectability which Capitalism ruthlessly destroys by poverty, except religion and the inborn sense of honour which has its citadel in the soul and can hold out (some times) against all circumstances.'[6]

This double standard is reflected in the Contagious Diseases Act of 1869 which subjected prostitutes to compulsory medical check-up without imposing periodic genital examination of their male clients. Plain-clothes policemen forced women to a humiliating internal examination every fortnight. The hypocrisy lies in justifying male sexual access to a class of fallen women while penalizing women for the same offence. Military officers argued that compulsory examination of soldiers for venereal disease would demoralize them. Thus the C.D. Act reflects a new enthusiasm for state intervention into the lives of the unrespectable poor. Women sympathized with the helpless prostitutes and organised mass protest under the leadership of Joshepine Butler for repeal of the controversial CD. Act. In 1869 the Ladies National Association was formed. Its manifesto denounced the Act as a blatant example of sex discrimination and official sanction of male vice. Fortunately, the Acts were repealed between 1870 and 1886. Judith R. Walkowitz commented in *Prostitution and Victorian Society*: 'The political legacy of that conflict would cast its shadow over medico-legal policy as well as the feminist struggle through World War-I.'[7]

Among the Victorian women who championed women's causes Joshephine Butler was prominent. She did not defend the 'right women;' she fought for the rights of the destitutes and prostitutes. She found her mission at the Brownlow Hill Workhouse where women and children lived in dingy and noisy cellars and often took to prostitution in desperation. Out of Liverpool's street-walking population of 9000, 1500 were under fifteen, and five hundred under thirteen. The age of consent was as low as twelve.

Joshephine Butler prayed with them, nursed the sick in their dark dens and often took the saddest cases to her home. Her fame spread as she began to seek employment for the girls she had rescued. Much before Bernard Shaw she had realized the economics of every day morality. To Joshepine Butler every woman, should enjoy four rights—the right to earn, to be educated, to decide the condition of her life by exercising the vote and the right to own the money she earned. Her blood boiled at the discriminatory principle of the C.D. Act and she thought it a crime to examine women against their will. She published an indictment entitled *The Constitution Violated*. She highlighted violation of law because the public mind would not think much of the physical violation of harlots. If women had the franchise, she argued, the Contagious Diseases Act could not have been passed. She became the President of the Ladies Association for the Repeal of C.D. Acts. Later she resigned from the presidency of her Council for Women's Higher Education as she could not lead both. Many of her educated friends deplored her choice: eminent persons such as Rev. Frederick D. Maurice, first principal of Queen's College for Girls, John Morley, the editor of *The Fortnightly Review* had publicly supported the C.D. Acts. On December 31, 1869 she published the Association Manifesto of eight clauses containing her social philosophy from which she never deviated.

The legal position of the ordinary woman was no better. She did not enjoy equal status with men in respect of property and income. After marriage her property and income passed on to her husband. Shaw could ridicule this exploitation only by setting the clock back two centuries in *The Devil's Disciple*. Set in 1777 he satirized women's powerlessness in a patriarchal culture and law. Mr. Dudgeon bequeathes an annuity to his wife out of the interest from her own income because as a married woman she has no control over her own property. She had even no right over her children. If her marriage proved to be unhappy due to drunkenness and cruelty of the husband, it was almost impossible to obtain divorce. The Custody of Infant Act, 1839, gave the mother the right of custody of children under 7. In 1873 the age of children was raised to 16. In 1855 Barbara Leigh Smith set up a committee to fight for stronger legal rights of women. Though under social pressure the Divorce Act of 1857 made divorce easier to obtain, it was guilty of double standard: a husband could obtain divorce on grounds of adultery alone, but a wife only for adultery with cruelty and desertion. It was not till 1923 that a woman could divorce her husband for adultery alone.

A husband was legally responsible for his wife's crime on the assumption that women did everything at their husband's bidding and were incapable of autonomous action. The Married Women's Property Act of 1870 allowed wives to keep their own property before and after marriage. These Acts made women financially less dependent and vulnerable to exploitation by mercenary husbands.

Women were also exploited in their workplace. The 1861 Census revealed that one third of manual labourers were women. They did hard physical work in mills, as dressmakers, shop assistants and domestic maid-servants for as long as 90 hours a week. Their wage was about one third of the average male wage. They were exploited in the sweated industries working long hours for paltry wages. Most women workers were not organised into trade unions. Married women were expected to do household work and bring up children as their additional duty. The 1901 Census revealed that there were 212 Lady doctors, two architects and a few clerks but many careers were still closed to women.

In Bryant and May's Match Factory in London poor match-girls worked for 10 hours a day for as little as 10 shillings a week. They ate their food in the workshop where phosphorus used in match production rotted their teeth and jaws. As a result of intervention by Annie Besant, the Management dismissed one of the workers' leaders. The match girls strongly retaliated by striking work and fighting with determination which forced the Management to improve their work conditions substantially.

The greatest obstacle to women's liberation was the lack of the right to vote. This cause was taken up by John Stuart Mill who argued eloquently in favour of perfect equality of sexes and women's right to vote in *The Subjection of Women* (1869). Mill argued unequivocally that 'Under whatever conditions and within whatever limits, men are admitted to the suffrage, there is not a shadow of justification for not admitting the women under the same.'[8]

As for women's entry to the professions and education Mill recommended the opening of all honourable employments and related training and educational facilities to women. Mill's attitude to women was much influenced by his intimate and lasting friendship with Mrs. Harriet Taylor, the wife of John Taylor and mother of two sons. They travelled together sharing each other's thoughts and ideas during weekends. In 1849 after a steady relationship for twenty years, the premature death of John Taylor made their marriage possible. To translate his belief in women's vote into a reality, Mill agreed to contest parliamentary election and after being elected presented a petition in favour of women's suffrage with fifteen hundred signatures. He saw the necessity of amending Disraeli's Reform Bill of 1867 to read 'person' in place of 'man'. He gave top priority to women's problems. In his will he left £6000, nearly half his property, to women's education. On Mill's death Lydia Becker extolled him as the person who dealt the first effectual blow at the political slavery of women.

A feminist movement grew under the leadership of women like Sophia Jex Blake, Joshephine Butler, Millicent Fawcett, Emmeline Pethick-Lawrence and others who drew their inspiration from Mary Wollstonecraft's *A Vindication of the Rights of Woman* (1792). After John Stuart Mill's debate in parliament on giving vote to women Lydia Becker founded the Manchester Women's Suffrage Committee which gradually developed into the National Union of Women's Suffrage Society (NUWSS). This society actively campaigned for suffrage for women on the same footing as men but was frustrated by government's lack of positive response. In 1888 women acquired the right to vote in the county council and could become parish and district councillors. Mrs. Emeline Pankhurst, the leader of the suffragette movement, and her daughters solicited support from the Liberal party but were disappointed by its apathy. In 1903 they formed the Women's Social and Political Union and resolved that militant action and a lot of publicity were the only means to secure votes. Members of WSPU vigorously questioned politicians in public meetings about their opinion on women suffrage.

They started shouting slogans and interrupting their public meetings by displaying flags and banners. As neither the Conservatives nor the Liberals would consent to votes for women, the frustrated suffragists resorted to breaking windows of government offices, burning empty buildings and blowing up a railway station. In 1912 Mrs. Pankhurst and hundreds of suffragettes were arrested. When they went on hunger-strike, they were forcibly fed through the nose with help of pipes. As the government was apprehensive about the possible death of hunger strikers, it passed a new legislation in 1913 which empowered the administration to release the suffragettes temporarily and then rearrest them after they had taken food and rest at home. This cunning measure came to be called the "Cat and Mouse Act." During a Campaign a well-known suffragette Emily Davison was knocked down and killed by the King's horse in Derby. This was reported as an accident by the anti-suffragist newspaper but the members of WSPU canonized her as a martyr and organised a massive demonstration in her honour.

The brutal way women were treated betrayed the falsity of the sentimental image that they were too pure and delicate to understand the rough world of politics. Many thought women were creatures of impulse and emotion, and were incapable of deciding questions on the basis of reason and logic. When World War I began in 1914, the suffragettes proved their rationality by suspending their agitation and helping the country cope with the crisis. As able-bodied men joined the army their work in factories and offices was taken up by women. After the dust of the war settled, the 1918 Act gave women over thirty the vote and the right to sit in parliament. But they had to wait for another decade to acquire the right to vote at the same age as men. Women were treated as second-class human beings, not just second-class citizens because they enjoyed no rights of the citizens.

Among the women who helped forward the women's cause by their outstanding contribution was Florence Nightingale. Lytton Strachey gave us the formidable character of a hitherto sentimentalized 'angel of mercy.' Florence's mother tried to engage her in household management without success. Her first and last choice was nursing work but her parents violently objected to her taking training in nursing. Richard Monckton Milnes proposed to her but she turned him down. In 1853 she was appointed superintendent of what she called 'a sanatarium for sick Governesses run by a committee of Five Ladies,' and within six months it was running efficiently. When cholera broke out in red-light district of London she nursed the prostitutes in a Middlesex Hospital. Her tireless and dedicated service to the women soldier and rare administrative ability have immortalized her as 'the Lady with the Lamp.'

On the literary horizon, the first important work on women's liberation was Mary Wollstonecraft's *A Vindication of the Rights of the Women* (1792). Before Wollstonecraft there was no systematic study of women's problems from economic and political perspectives. In her introduction she proposed to write with 'energetic emotions' and direct her arguments to the middle class women as she lives in a 'natural state'. By contrast the aristocratic woman is spoiled by great wealth and is incapable of any redemption by education, she says 'We shall not see women affectionate till more equality be established in society, till ranks are confounded and women freed.'[9]

Wollstonecraft was aware that the women she was addressing might be disinclined to follow her hard logic. Yet she hoped to reach a few ambitious and courageous women like herself. *A Vindication* examined closely how early environmental influences shaped the character of girls. She refused to accept the age-old belief that women were born inferior to men and added that superficial changes in women's condition, alleviation of isolated grievances or the creation of a few elites were not the right way to solve the problem. Shaw too regarded women's bondage as a cultural construct which they took as natural. He strikes at the root of this deep-seated conditioning. In *Intelligent Woman's Guide* he writes, 'If a woman has been accustomed to go in chains all her life and to see other women doing the same, a proposal to take her chains off will horrify her. It is easier to put chains on people than to take them off if the chains look respectable.'[10]

Wollstonecraft was angry because she thought women themselves were responsible for their bondage: their ignorance and uselessness provided fuel to the anti-feminists. She pointed out how girls are encouraged by their parents and teachers to conform to feminine ideals of modesty and dependence. Against domestic drudgery she complained that constant companionship among sisters, mother, and in-laws denied them the solitude necessary for mental growth. Though Wollstonecraft sympathised with the political ideas of Jean Jacques Rousseau, she would not accept his traditional opinion about women's inferiority. Rousseau's 'Sophie' is the antithesis of her rational woman. She is inherently weak and exists only to provide entertainment to men. She described the attempt to raise women on high pedestal as confining them to cages like the feathered race with mock majesty from perch to perch. She looked upon romantic love as an arbitrary passion, a stalking mischief, the opposite of reason which cannot last long in marriage without exhausting itself.

Wollstonecraft asserted that a women's first duty is to herself and whenever any conflict is perceived between domestic duties and reason, it is reason which should be served. She subscribed to the idea of women's responsibility as mother and recommended education for this purpose. The main thesis of Wollstonecraft is educating women to be independent and useful. Earning one's living is the foundation of all virtue. The ideal woman portrayed in *A Vindication* is active and intelligent, blending civic and family responsibilities, free from drudgery and economic dependence. Wollstonecraft envisaged the emergence of a new world: 'It is time to effect a revolution in female manners—time to restore to them their lost dignity—and make them, as a part of human species, labour by reforming themselves to reform the world.'[11] *In the Intelligent Woman's Guide to Socialism and Capitalism*. Shaw writes in the same vein:

> 'At present a married woman is the female slave enchained to a male one; and a girl is a prisoner in the house and in the hands of her parents. When the personal relation between the parties is affectionate, and their powers not abused, the arrangement works well enough to be bearable by people who have been brought up to regard it as a matter of course. But when the parties are selfish, tyrannical, jealous, cruel, envious, with different and

antagonistic tastes and beliefs, incapable of understanding one another: in short antipathetic and incompatible, it produces untold human unhappiness.

Why is this unhappiness endured when the door is not locked, and the victims can walk into the street at any moment? Obviously because starvation awaits them at the other side of the door. Vows and inculcated duties may seem effective in keeping unhappy wives and revolting daughters at home when they have no alternative; but there must be an immense number of cases in which wives and husbands, girls and boys, would walk out of the house, like Nora Helmer in Ibsen's famous play, if they could do so without losing a single meal, a single night's protection and shelter, or any of their social standing in consequence.'[12]

He believed that only socialism could liberate men and women from such slavery. Therefore, he remained a champion of socialism till the end of his life.

On the theatrical front an accomplished actress and writer named Elizabeth Robins became famous for her roles as Ibsen's Hedda and Hilda. Later she abandoned her stage career to write plays, novels and articles to further the cause of the suffrage movement. After the success of her play *Votes for Women* at the Court Theatre in 1907, she turned to organizing the Actresses French League and took charge of Women Writers' Suffrage League. The 'new woman' became the protagonist of Ibsen and Rebecea West's plays.

Though the plays under review do not profess to give a parallel picture of women's struggle for emancipation, they articulate a new consciousness: the polemics about women's status in society. There is a strong undercurrent in the early plays of Shaw and Granville Barker, and the late plays of Galsworthy that without women's emancipation the improvement of humanity would ever remain incomplete. Much of their advanced ideas anticipated the feminist consciousness of Simone de Beauvoir, Betty Friedan and Germaine Greer.

Indeed, with the appearance of Ibsen's *Pillars of Society* in 1877 began a new wave and in England it thrived with the publication of Shaw's *Widowers' Houses* in 1892. Gone are the passive heroines in their soul-destroying domestic role of the 'female eunuchs'. A new breed of assertive and intellectual women, who are dissatisfied with their built-in servile status, appear on the stage and set out to bring about a radical change in their lives. They behaved unconventionally like Ann and andida, asked subversive uestions about the basic assumptions about the man-woman relationship like ina, esbia and Ann eete sometimes they turned the tables on the male egotists.

In their revolutionary spirit they resembled their real-life counterparts rs. ankhurst, ydia ecker, eatrice ebb and George Eliot. They e hibit a rare courage to carry out their intellectual convictions. istorically they belong to the first women's liberation movement but their spirit and ideas are far ahead of their time. Their motivation to bring about a transformation from within anticipates the more assertive feminism of the 197 s.

The success of the first feminist movement was only partial. omen won the vote but the basic social structure or the uality of their life remained more or less the same. In .S.A. Emma Goldman lectured brilliantly on Shaw, Ibsen and Strindberg, edited the anarchist monthly *ot er art* advocating changes in women's position in relation to marriage, child-rearing and se ual fulfilment. In her autobiography she has recorded how she flatly turned down the proposal of a r. because she had no intention of being chained to a man forever.'[1] She argued that in addition to economic independence a women should en oy the right of maintaining a loving relationship with a man and re oice in motherhood without the bondage of marriage. The idea of marriage and family was considered a detriment to women's development but almost a century later even firebrand feminist like etty riedan admits in *e Seco d Sta e* that having achieved success in career and economic freedom, some women complain about a 'devastating loneliness' due to an unmitigated desire to have a house, a garden and a kid. They think the women's movement is responsible for making the family an 'endangered species.'[14] Even this avant-garde idea appeared in the 'new drama' a decade ago. Violet created a scandal by being pregnant yet refusing to reveal the name of her child's father in Shaw's *Man and Superman*. A parallel story is unfolded in Granville Barker's *The Madras House* in which Miss Marion Yates defies her employer by her obdurate refusal to divulge the name of her child's father. In both cases they asserted their right to be mothers without first being wives.

After a century when women hold the highest offices of prime minister, chief justice, surgeon and university professor, the revolutionary ideas if the 'New Woman' and her achievements are likely to be underestimated. Nevertheless it remains an unalterable fact that the emergence of the "New Woman" precipitated the exit of the romantic heroine so long worshipped on a pedestal and weary of playing the vapid role of the sacrificing mother and docile wife.

Women's crusade for self-liberation began with Lona Hessel's symbolic declaration at the end of Act I of *Pillars of Society* (1877); 'I want to let in some fresh air, my dear Pastor'[15] and culminates in the triumph of the transformed flower-girl Eliza over her megalomaniac mentor Prof. Higgins who is forced to acknowledge in Shaw's *Pygmalion*, (1913): 'Five minutes ago you were like a millstone round my neck. Now you're a tower of strength: a consort battleship.'[16] The improvement in woman's status become all the more obvious when we compare Eliza's victory with Catherine's humiliating submission in Shakespeare's *The Taming of the Shrew*.

II

The dramatic innovations and experiments of the last decade of nineteenth century England owe much to the naturalistic technique of Zola and the social realism of Ibsen. The newness of the 'new drama' lies in its unconvential morality which is represented by the New Woman. In the Greek drama we have a few daring heroines like Antigone and Medea. Female sexuality is regarded a threat to male domination. The heroic daughter of king Oedipus, Antigone is determined to perform the last rights of burial of her anarchist brother in violation to the end and does not allow obstacles to undermine her courage and conviction. But with her death the new morality succumbs to state authority. Phaedra commits suicide in *Hyppolytus* after falling in love with her stepson. In *Agamemnon* Clytemnestra is charged with treason and subversion. Female chastity was glorified in Elizabethan drama. The wit of Portia and Rosalind end up in marriage.

Euripide's Medea lacks the intellectual conviction of Sophocles' heroine. Medea's strength lies in her passion and her single-minded devotion. She reacts violently to her lover's cold indifference and finally revenges herself by killing his second wife and her own children. The final impression is that of a tragic woman waylaid by her jealousy and frustration. Despite her courage the Greek heroine falls short of a superwoman.

The Greek heroine who comes closer to the Shavian intellectual woman is Lysistrata, the protagonist of *Lysistrata*, a comedy written by Aristophanes in 411 B.C. With a name which means 'one who disbands armies' she reveals her leadership quality of strategic thinking by convening a meeting of women to form a coalition to prevent war. This awareness of women's power gives her control over women as well as men. Women, she suggested, should starve their men sexually till they give up fighting, and the matrons of Athens should cut off the financial support to the military. Their oath to eradicate war and promote peace is finally crowned with success when the belligerent men of both Athens and Sparta join hands to fight against their common enemy. How the male ego was hurt is shown in the behaviour of the city magistrate who ordered her arrest but was eventually won over by her polemics for peace.

In Elizabethan England John Webster created a determined protagonist in *The Duchess of Malfi*. A spirited and high-minded widow, the duchess shows unusual temerity of character by marrying the honest steward Antonio in defiance of the warnings of her brothers who wanted to usurp her inheritance.

She suffers persecution and embraces death rather than give up her lover. Granville Barker took up the theme of marriage between lovers of unequal status in *The Marrying of Ann Leete* and turned it into a comedy.

In Shakespeare's *Coriolanus* Volumnia, the mother of the hero dominates the play. She guides and advises her son in political matters. It is she who persuades him to spare Rome when Coriolanus is about to attack it as revenge for his banishment. In *The Merchant of Venice* and *As You Like It* Shakespeare created Portia and Rosalind who bring scintillating wit and intelligence to the romantic heroine. Another assertive heroine is Cleopatra but she fails to go beyond narrow self-interest. But these examples are exceptions rather than the rule and do not represent the contemporary trend. The New Woman was inducted into the modern drama by Henrik Ibsen. The assertive heroines of *Pillars of Society*, *A Doll's House*, *Ghosts*, *The Lady from the Sea*, *Hedda Gabler*, *Rosmersholm* and *The Master Builder* influenced the 'unwomanly woman' of Shaw and his contemporaries. Therefore, a brief critical study of the Ibsenite New Woman is a key to the understanding of the New Woman in the English Dramatic Revival (1890-1914).

Ibsen's modern play begins with the publication of *Pillars of Society* (1877). It is here for the first time that the complexity of social life receives a fresh treatment. Ibsen interweaves the question of women's status in society with a realistic treatment of corruption in public life. It is a play in which the sins of the pseudo-moralist anti-hero is expiated by the social outcastes—Lona Hessel, the New Woman, and her protegé Johan Tonnsen. In the anti-climactic ending the hero emerges as a poseur who deliberately used his social authority for private gain, and the scapegoats of scandal like Lona and Johan emerge as the true benefactors of mankind.

Critics have paid scant attention to the symbolic induction of the 'new drama' through Lona Hessel's speech at the close of the First Act: 'I want to let in some fresh air.' Lona lets in not just air, but a gale which sweeps away the worn-out conventional drama. The title of the play is truly symbolic. It revolves around the conflict between the hollow pillars, the mercenary do-gooders and the real pillars who take the brunt of their guilt and are maligned and disgraced in the process.

Though Ibsen has been acknowledged as the Father of modern drama, his greatest contribution—the New Woman as protagonist has hardly received the attention it deserves. Only James Joyce paid a brief compliment by pointing out that Ibsen's knowledge of humanity is nowhere more obvious than in his portrayal of women.[17] While critical studies of women characters of Shakespeare and Shaw abound, no eminent critic has made an exclusive study of Ibsen's heroines. A possible reason was Ibsen's refusal to be branded as a feminist. At a banquet held in his honour by the Norwegian society for Women's Rights in 1898, Ibsen disappointed the organisers by publicly disclaiming any connection with women's rights. He argued that he was concerned with the portrayal of human beings, and since women constituted approximately half of the population, their problems found a prominent place in his works.[18] But the plays speak louder than their creator: Ibsen was the first dramatist to treat the ordeals of womanhood and stir the public conscience by his polemics about her position in society. Ironically, Ibsen came to be associated with feminism. The debates and discussions grew so widespread that a notice had often to be put up in parties requesting visitors not to discuss Ibsen.

Of all the heroines of Ibsen, Nora is the most well-known, but it is Lona who truly embodies the new spirit. Her dissatisfaction with and fight against moral pretence and dead conventions is consistent with her aggressive role. The play is centred on the ideological conflict between a 'small' nation with narrow outlook represented by Bernick and Rorlund, and the 'big' world with broad outlook represented by Johan and Lona. Bernick and his coterie publicly set themselves up as pillars of society while they use their social influence to feather their nests. They vehemently oppose railway communication with the outside world on the pretext of moral pollution. Bernick is a typical puritan with a penchant for social respectability while at the same time tasting the forbidden fruit of an illicit Love. He manages to absolve himself from the scandalous love affair with Mrs. Dorf and the insolvency of his firm by using Johan as a scapegoat. But this manipulation does not succeed permanently.

The first blow comes from the 'New Woman'—Lona Hessel's rejection of the depraved Bernick who had courted her but later left her to marry her cousin Betty for money is like a slap on the face. Lona's slap, Nora's slamming the door are protests against men's exploitation of women for their advancement. Similar protest is seen in Mrs. Alving's decision to leave her debauched husband. In *The Lady from the Sea*, Ellida, the second wife of a kind and considerate doctor, shocks her complacent husband by her decision to depart with her former lover. She is, however cured of this infatuation only when she is allowed to act as a free agent. In Ibsen's world the male characters inwardly crave to escape the morbid influence of a puritan society but nevertheless perpetuate its hypocrisies. Women in general play the docile roles of dutiful daughters and sacrificing wives. Mrs. Solness talks incessantly about her duties. Betty Bernick is snubbed by her husband when she inquires about the proposed Railway scheme. Bernick allocates their role as 'help and a comfort to... nearest and dearest.[19] Dina Dorf is branded a moral delinquent because her mother had an extra-marital affair.

Lona Hessel's unexpected return from self-exile raises many eyebrows and upsets the relatives, and her respectable ex-lover. The white clothes women are sewing symbolize mourning and 'the moral linen smells bad ... just like a shroud'. Lona prescribes the remedy for a sick society: 'We'll soon get ourselves out of his tomb. Clear daylight is what's needed.'[20]

The self-appointed moral pillars grudge her further intrusion; but she becomes the unstoppable harbinger of a new freedom. Behaving magnanimously and eschewing rancour, she undertakes the most difficult task of reforming her former lover. The false pillar gives way under the impact of her strong personality. Bernick is forced to realize that he has not only misused public faith for his private profit but also has been trapped into a life of self-deception. His contact with this dominating personality instills courage in him to confess his past guilt. In the final Act when the citizens congregate to offer their profuse gratitude to Bernick, he stuns the world by narrating how he betrayed people's faith by purchase of the proposed site of the railway line for personal profit. He confesses his secret affair with Mrs. Dorf and spreading the rumour about stolen money to save his family prestige. The play ends with Bernick passing all credits to Lona: 'Women are the real pillars of society.[21] This climactic acknowledgement is a milestone in women's advancement in life as well as in the drama. Women's struggle for freedom is the recurrent theme of Ibsen's plays.

The choice to focus on women's bondage is not co-incidental. In the predicament of women Ibsen must have seen the plight of the repressed individual groaning under the weight of outdated attitudes and conventions. When Johan leaves the town to save Bernick's reputation, Lona goes along to take care of him. When he falls sick she sings in the cafés, gives lectures and writes a controversial book to meet the expenses. This fifteen years' struggle against a male-dominated culture makes her a tower of strength. But the women who stay in the back-waters of the town groan under the pressure of puritanism. Dina suffers from an inferiority complex due to her mother's scandalous affair and could never imagine herself anything better than a moral delinquent. Martha Bernick's efforts to achieve economic independence is frowned upon by her brother who could think of no better way of using her than 'to cope with things as they crop up.' Bernick assigns her role: 'She has plenty to interest her... me and Betty and Olaf and me. People should never think primarily of themselves, least of all women.'[22] In his scheme of things Martha has no place as an individual. He even boasts that his wife has no place as an individual: she has learnt to accommodate *her* nature to his way of thinking. This is the kind of built-in slavery and exploitation of women which Betty Friedan complained about in *The Feminine Mystique* (1963).

In a society where women's contribution is only grudgingly acknowledged, Lona achieves the impossible. Under her influence Bernick is forced to take stock of his private as well as public life. He no longer has the complacency of leading an examplary life for the citizens. With the realization that his life is built on a quagmire of lies and hypocrisy, he welcomes the beginning of a new era. He even admits that posing to be, 'a pillar of society is really irksome' and begs Lona to stay. She in her turn indicts society for his moral degeneration: 'The society of yours is like a lot of old bachelors: you never see the women.'[23]

The theme of women's awakening has further been reinforced by the subplot of the Dina-Johan love affair. Dina, the victim of her mother's scandal, too realizes the futility of self-sacrifice and responds to Johan's call for a life of fulfilment. She musters the courage to reject her fiancé and moral guardian Rorlund for his condescending attitude. It is not just a change of spouse, it is a change of outlook. She seeks Johan's help to find work and become economically independent—the corner stone of true freedom. Martha too is infected with this new wave of liberation, she laments: 'Oh the tyranny of all this convention, doing the right thing, how we are made to suffer under it here.'[24]

Her decisive role makes her the protagonist—the real pillar, and the anti-hero pales. And this trend continues in *A Doll's House*, *Ghosts*, *The Lady from the Sea* and *Rosmersholm*. The need for individual freedom is the central theme of these plays. The bondage of domestic duty and an uncritical acceptance of social respectability are the real stumbling blocks to the growth and maturity of the heroine's personality. Their struggle within a patriarchal culture is a process of emancipation by ordeal. *A Doll's House* is chiefly a study of women's status within marriage. Nora is Everywoman. Her bondage and subservient status is evident from her unsuspecting acceptance of pet names like 'little squirrel' 'little spendthrift' 'little skylark' given by her condescending husband, implying a relationship between a patron and protegé. It is fear and deference that lead Nora to suppress her act of forging her father's signature to raise an emergent loan for her husband's medical treatment. Nora overstrains herself to pay off this secret loan and even spends agonizing days under the threat of a black-mailer, expecting her husband to be grateful for such a sacrifice.

The real point of the play is Nora's growth from Everywoman in the First Act to a New woman in the last. Her revolt is two-fold: she refuses to live with a husband who withdraws his support at the greatest crisis of her life. She also revolts against the biased law which precludes a wife from raising a loan on her own. Her best efforts to play the ideal wife and mother is thwarted by Krogstad a black-mailer who wants to retain his job at Helmer's bank even after the detection of his forgery.

Nora, despite her most assertive and mature decision, is a long-term victim of patriarchal culture. Her subordinate status is to some extent her own making: She delights in puerile epithets like 'little songbird' 'little rogue' and always strives to live up to her husband's taste and expectation. It is only at the moment of her greatest trial that she realizes that her overprotective husband would not share the disgrace of her scandalous forgery. Thus the deferential Nora develops into a mature woman in search of an identity. She spurns every offer of reconciliation with her egotist husband as realization dawns on her that a real marriage based on equal status and mutual respect is impossible—'a miracle of miracles.'

A Doll's House created such a commotion that Ibsen chose a somewhat softer stance to public sentiment in *Ghosts*. Mrs. Alving, the protagonist of the play, is an intellectual wife with advanced ideas. She revolts against her husband's debauchery with the maid-servant and her subsequent pregnancy. But her determination to leave her husband is foiled by the intervention of her past lover Pastor Mandes, an upholder of social respectability. This New Woman was certainly bolder than her contemporaries but not bold enough to transcend the conventional morality of her time.

Her life turns into a tragedy when she discovers with horror that her son Oswald has inherited not only his father's veneral diseases, but also his passion and *joi de vivre* which finds expression in the incestuous relationship with his half-sister. Though she gradually learns to accept such unconventional behaviour, the ghosts of dead ideas and her adherence to conventional morality turn her life into a misery and smother her desire for emancipation. The Pastor persuades her to stay with her depraved husband and she succumbs. When Nora slammed the door respectable society screamed. So Mrs. Alving is made to bow to social codes and conventions which ultimately destroy her. In desperation she cries: 'Oh! Ideals! Ideals! If I weren't such a coward.'[25] Thus Mrs. Alving's tragic waste proves the futility of a biased moral code.

The freedom which Mrs. Alving fails to achieve in *Ghosts* is attained by Ellida, the assertive heroine of *The Lady from the Sea*. In this play of psychological subtleties Ibsen creates a slightly neurotic woman who attains her independent status within marriage only through a war of nerves with her husband. As a doll wife like Nora she feels unhappy, useless and without responsibility. Her inner struggle against this life of an ineffectual captive finds expression in her neurotic obsession with a sea-faring lover with whom she had a mock-marriage in the past. The return of this lover revives the spell on her and leads to the climax when she must make the most important decision of her life: whether to continue her present meaningless existence or to quit with her past lover. Dr. Wangal's efforts to help her out of this crisis fail. Only when she is given absolute freedom to choose, is this mysterious spell broken. She rejects the lover and stays with her family. In this psychoanalytic play before the advent of Freudian theory, Ibsen emphasizes women's need for freedom as the essential condition for the growth and happiness of personality. Incidentally, Ellida is based on a real woman and a feminist named Camilla Collet.

As a realist Ibsen portrays not only the triumph of the newly-won freedom but also the tragedy of its abuse. Having attained her rights a woman may forget her duties. A wife prematurely emancipated can become a *femme fatale*. In *Hedda Gabler* the liberated wife of Tessman destroys her lover and herself in her pursuit of power. Hedda's friend Thea leaves her old lover Lovborg and leads him to enviable intellectual height. Driven by jealousy at her success and bored by her unexciting life with her scholarly husband, she takes sadistic delight in goading Lovborg to suicide by offering her pistol. Her machiavellian plan succeeds only temporarily, giving way to greater depression when she discovers that Thea has managed to inspire her husband with the same dedication towards the noble task of publishing Lovorg's *magnum opus*. Hedda's obsessive urge to control her men's lives subjects her to more and more desperation and finally to her tragic self-annihilation.

Perverse imagination leads another *femme fatale* astray in *The Master Builder*. Like Hedda, Hilda Wangel destroys the man she adored as a child. Under her spell Solness behaves like a puppet. She seduces the master-builder to climb the scaffolding on the high tower just to fulfil her dream. The ageing architect embraces death under the influence of the neurotic *enfant terrible* whom Shaw calls a 'tiny animal'[26] in *The Quintessence of Ibsenism*.

In *Rosmersholm* Ibsen has delineated an intellectual woman of unconventional morality, Rebecca West who overreaches herself in her passion to lead Rosmer to advanced ideas and the cause of liberation. Her initial influence helps Rosmer to outgrow his useless life of drudgery and obsolete beliefs. A woman of great promise, she ends up as a tragic woman, having resorted to petty means to achieve the noble end.

Her selfless love and concern for Rosmer's development leads her to destroy his wife with the false rumour about her pregnancy. But after her death she discovers with astonishment that her passion has ebbed away. Rebecca who came to reform Rosmer is in great need of edification herself. She acknowledges her gratitude to Rosmer and prepares to go back to her native place. Rosmer realizes the truth that 'human beings cannot be ennobled from without.' As retribution for their sin they drown themselves in the millstream of Rosmersholm. Rebecca is Ibsen's superwoman wasted. When liberated women set out to rob their men's freedom, they have then no better fate than their tyrannical male counterparts.

If Ibsen shows women's oppression and their struggle for emancipation, Shaw unfolds their potential as well as attainment. His indebtedness to Ibsen is revealed in *The Philanderer*, a play about a 'New Woman' written in 1893 for the Independent Theatre when, according to Shaw, not only dramatic literature but life itself was staggering from the impact of Ibsen's plays. After almost four decades he added a prefatory note in which he still maintained: 'The human nature in it is still in the latest fashion: indeed I am far more sure that its ideas, instead of being 36 years behind the times, are not for a considerable section of the community 36 years ahead of them'[27] Without Ibsen, Shaw's superwomen would have been inconceivable. The New Women inducted into the plays of Shaw, Granville Barker and Galsworthy changed the character of drama: Women's status in society and their problems were discussed; their struggle for emancipation within a patriarchal culture effectively portrayed, and women occupy centre stage as protagonists. The assertive heroines of modern drama as equal partners owe their status to the efforts of Shaw and his contemporaries. Of course Shaw's feminism is not free from limitations and controversies. His glorification of motherhood in *Man and Superman* was frowned upon by a section of feminists for the obvious reason that pressures of motherhood make women's participation almost impossible. But there are diehard feminists like Betty Friedan who have come a long way from their uncompromising stand to acknowledge the need for motherhood and family life. In *The Second Stage* (1983) she says: 'The second stage involves coming to new terms with the family—new terms with love and with work. The second stage may not even be a women's movement. Men may be at the cutting edge of the second stage. The second stage has to transcend the battle for equal power in institution.'[28]

NOTES AND REFERENCES

1. Bernard Shaw, *The Intelligent Woman's Guide to Socialism and Capitalism* (London, Constable & Co., 1928), p. 197.
2. G.M. Young, *Victorian England: Portrait of an Age* (London, O.U.P. 1936), p. 23.

3. Shaw: *The Intelligent Woman*, p. 199.
4. *Twenty-four One-Act Plays* (London, J.M. Dent, 1938), p. 161.
5. Virgina Woolf, *A Room of One's Own* (London, Chatto & Windus, 1984), p. 33.
6. Shaw: *The Intelligent Woman*, p. 201.
7. Judith R. Walkowitz, *Prostitution and Victorian Society* (Cambridge, Cambridge, Un 1980), p. 80.
8. J.S. Mill *The Subjection of Women* (Cambridge, M.I.T. Press, 1970), p. 16.
9. Mary Wollstonecraft, *A Vindication of the Rights of the Women* (Hermondsworth, Penguin, 1978), p. 72.
10. Shaw: *The Intelligent Woman's Guide*, p. 406.
11. Wollstonecraft: *A Vindication*, p. 123.
12. *The Intelligent Woman's Guide*, p. 408.
13. *Living My Life*, Vol. I (New York, Dover Publication, 1970), p. 229.
14. Betty Friedan, *The Second Stage* (London, Abacus, 1983), pp. 20-21.
15. James Walter MacFarlane, ed. & tr., *Ibsen: Plays* (Bombay, O.U.P., 1975), p. 28.
16. Bernard Shaw, *The Complete Plays of Bernard Shaw* (London, Paul Hamlyn, 1965), p. 751. All quotations of Shaw's plays are from this edition which is henceforth abbreviated to 'Shaw: Plays'
17. Michael Egan, ed., *Henrik Ibsen: Critical Heritage* (London, Routledge & K.P., 1972), p. 388.
18. Michael Meyer, *Henrik Ibsen: The Making of a Dramatist* (London, Rupert Hart Davis, 1971), p. 266.
19. Ibsen: *Plays*, p. 21.
20. *Ibid.*, p. 27.
21. *Ibid.*, p. 106.
22. *Ibid.*, p. 46.
23. *Ibid.*, p. 106.
24. *Ibid.*, p. 86.
25. Eva Le Gallienne, Ed., *Six Plays by Henrik Ibsen* (N. York, Modern Library, 1957), p. 117.

26. Bernard Shaw, *The Quintessence of Ibsenism* (London, Constable, 1913), p. 126.
27. Bernard Shaw, *The Complete Prefaces of Bernard Shaw* (London, Paul Hamlyn, 1965), p. 835.
28. Betty Friedan, *The Second Stage* (London, Abacus, 1983), p. 28.

SHAW: THE NEW WOMAN AS VITAL GENIUS

3

I

The plays of the dramatic revival (1890-1914) were remarkable for many reasons. The literary production of this time is steeped in realism which faithfully reflected not only the spirit of the age but its problems also. Literature, and drama in particular, being imitations of action, represent life. Their affinity is most aptly analogized by Shakespeare in *As You Like it*: 'All the world's a stage, And all the men and women merely players....' (II.7.139). Though the sociological value of literature is great, no writer can express society completely and exhaustively. It is not a reflection of total social process but the essence of all history. The interaction between the artist and society is of great importance. In every age the eminent intellectuals are the trend-setters. The writer is not only influenced by society: he influences it. Art not only reproduces life but also shapes it. People may model their lives upon the patterns of fictional heroes and heroines. As realism or naturalism dominated the literary convention, so did the moral purpose influence the themes of the dramatic revival. The drama became a vehicle of the intellectual preoccupations of the day.

One of the outstanding preoccupations was the Woman Question. Under the influence of Ibsen, Shaw set a new trend by inducting the New Woman into his early and middle plays and gave her the central role. His contemporary Granville Barker showed the struggle of the New Woman within patriarchal culture. A shift in gender bias is also noticeable in the late plays of John Galsworthy. Their plays not only show women's plight in a male-dominated culture, but an underlying motive to improve their status. If Ibsen has portrayed woman's struggle, these playwrights show the fruits of their endeavour—the changing status and some modest gains. For the first time in drama women outgrow their object-like status to become the real subject. The Independent Theatre founded by J.T. Grein in 1891 was used by these dramatists to stage their serious plays.

Their predecessors, Arthur Wing Pinero and Henry Arthur Jones only made some half-hearted attempts to deal with the theme of woman's emancipation in 'society drama' but their conventional outlook and desire to perpetuate Victorian morality prevented them from creating the new drama. In *The Liars* (1897) Jones smothered the flame of discontent in his heroine, Lady Jessica Nepean and forced her to seek her husband's forgiveness. *Mrs Dane's Defence* (1900) ends with the rejection of a woman with a past. The heroine of *The Case of Rebellious Susan* (1894) begins as a feminist debunking marriage as 'a hateful wretched institution' and leaves her husband to punish unfaithfulness. But a repressive society forces her to retreat with the conclusion. 'You see, dear, we poor women cannot retaliate.'[1] Like Jones, Pinero also showed some concern for women's problems but he too catered to the conventional morality of his audience. In his plays women of promise degenerated into weak and shallow characters. Mrs Posket conceals her age to her second husband. Iris degrades herself. Rose Trelawany is forced to reconcile with her fiancé whom she had rejected earlier. The emancipated heroine of *The Notorious Mrs Ebsmith* (1895) deviates from her idea and wastes her life. Any deviation from the moral strait-jacket is ruthlessly punished.

More priggish are the melodramatic suicides of Mrs Tanqueray and Zoe Blundell. *The Second Mrs. Tanqueray* unfolds the unsuccessful struggle of a woman with a past to return to the mainstream. The happiness of her conjugal life is marred by her step-daughter Ellen who ironically falls in love with a person who 'kept house together' with her. When her past affair comes to light, Ellen condemns Mrs Tanqueray in the harshest language driving her to deep despair and self-pity. Despite her husband's sympathy, this 'worn-out creature' 'a ghost, a wreck' 'tainted through and through' finds her life ruined by the scandal. Pinero's attitude is well expressed through Aubrey's comment of her death: 'My poor wretched wife! My poor wretched wife.' A drama that began as a social criticism ended up as a sentimental tragedy for the moral edification of women. A parallel is found in *Mid channel* which explores the mid-life crisis of a couple after thirteen years of marriage. While both the husband and the wife carry on extra-marital affairs, it is the wife who remains unforgiven and finally driven to suicide. Pinero failed because he could never transcend Victorian double standards.

The husband of Zoe Blundell would not condone his wife's affair while he treats his own as a male privilege. And the convent-educated daughter of Mrs Tanquery would not forgive the promiscuous behaviour of her mother which she so easily overlooks in her lover. In the original text the final speech by Drummle sums up the dismal picture of women's position:

> And I—I've been hard on this woman! Good God, men are on all women![2]

Oscar Wilde with all his brilliant wit and intellect fares no better. Like Pinero and Jones he too reinforced the vulnerability of the Victorian women and supremacy of men. In *Lady Windermere's Fan* (1892) the divorced mother Mrs Erlynne comes to the rescue of the daughter when her fan is discovered in her lover's room, by pretending to have borrowed it. But in a similar scandalous affair in *An Ideal Husband* (1895) the wife is advised by her family friend to forgive her husband to save him from black-mailing by his former mistress. *A Woman of No Importance*, (1893) however, has a strong female character as protagonist. Mrs Arbuthnot not only disapproves of her son being her former lover's secretary but also humiliates him by revealing the identity of her son when he slaps him for taking liberties with his fiancée. Yet Mrs Arbuthnot's personal victory over her male antagonist can hardly be seen as a victory for her sex.

In sharp contrast to this scenario of women as victims of undeserved suffering and unrealized aspirations, Shaw introduced his heroines as winners. As a Fabian socialist Shaw perceived that like the working-class, women were grossly exploited. So, concentrating on their problems would advance the cause of socialism which alone could help them realize their potential and attain equality. In his speeches, articles, letters and prefaces he showed an awareness of and involvement with the women's problems which would earn him the status of a specialist. He even wrote two topical plays *Fanny's First Play* and *Press Cuttings* when the movement of women's suffrage was at its peak in Edwardian England.

Shaw's view on women's emancipation is not only original but also far ahead of his time. As a socialist intellectual he supported the suffragist's demand for vote on equal terms. As early as 1884 Shaw drafted the Fabian Manifesto, Tract no 2 which recognised women's rights and asserted '...that Men no longer need special political privileges to protect them against women: and that the sexes should henceforth enjoy equal political right.' Later in 1907 in his 'Draft or Propositions on which to Found a Revised Basis' Shaw further wrote: 'The Fabian society not only aims at complete equality as between the sexes, but at their economic independence. It advocates the explicit recognition by legally secured rights or payments of the value of the domestic work of women to their immediate partners and to the state as house-keepers, child-bearers, nurses and matrons.'

As a friend and sympathizer of Mrs Pankhurst and her followers he strongly criticized the Asquith government for the unjustified arrests under the vindictive Cat and Mouse Act and its inhuman treatment of the suffragists. His letters and articles of protest were published in feminist papers like *Votes for Women* and Suffragette. His *Man and Superman* was hailed by Mrs Pankhurst as an inspiring play which strengthened her purpose and fortified her courage. On November 12, 1915 Shaw suggested through *Votes for Women* that the best way of paying homage to Edith Cavell would be by enfranchising her sex in recognition of her valour and sacrifice.

Shaw's contribution to the suffragist cause was best recognized by the old suffragist who stood outside the building holding the flag of the suffragettes at his funeral at Golders Green crematorium in November, 1950. To the critics who consider Shaw out of date and 'old hat', Rodelle Weintraub, the editor of *Fabian Feminist: Shaw and Woman* points out that '... much of Shaw is not only still fresh but can be seen in the banners and goals of contemporary feminist movement: equal opportunity to secure employment and equal pay for equal work; contracts for marriage; marriage free from degrading economic and possessive sexual factors; dignified divorce; financial freedom with or without marriage; ownership of property exclusive of one's husband; the bearing of children outside of marriage and the refusal to bear children; equal opportunity to participate in atheletics; legal equality of every variety.'[3]

In his public statement about women's suffrage, Shaw was never patronising; he appealed to the reason of thinking men that women deserved the vote as a fundamental right. He argued that women could not be proved to be more politically immature, socially prejudiced, narrow-minded and selfish than men. Like men they are intelligent enough to know when they are uncomfortable. Almost a century before the concept of Human Resource Development came into being, Shaw regretted that woman as a valuable resource was being wasted:

> '... all that talent that women have now instead of being applied to the solution of social problems .... is wasted in this agitation—an agitation which ought to be utterly unnecessary because women are struggling to get franchise.'[4]

He pointed out that by giving franchise to women England would channel an immense flood of political and social energy and both sexes would work as a team to solve social problems. The basis of Shavian polemics is equality of the sexes—a belief he cherished all his life. In his married life Shaw respected Charlotte's wish to live without a sexual relationship. Moreover, she ate meat and drank whiskey while Shaw remained a strict vegetarian and a teetotaller. He refused to file a joint income tax return in compliance with British Law because it would imply a wife's lack of identity. He also thought it improper to know his wife's income and requested the tax authorities to ascertain it for themselves.

Shaw strongly protested against the imprisonment and forcible feeding of Mrs Codben-Sanderson, the leader of the Women's Movement and daughter of Richard Codben. In *The Times*, 31st October, 1906, he wrote how he was shocked to see 'one of the nicest women of England suffering from the coarsest indignity and the most injurious form of ill-treatment that law could inflict on a pick-pocket.'

He was also outraged by Herbert Gladstone's view that forcible feeding was not painful. He threw an open challenge to him in *The Times*, 23 November, 1909, to accept a free dinner in which his partaking of delicacies through the nose would be cinematographically recorded to convince the public that such feeding was innocuous.

But Shaw was nothing if not paradoxical. He loved publicity through controversial opinions and delighted in attacking beliefs which people held sacred. In an interview with Maud Churton in 1906 he said that suffrage meant nothing to him as he had already got it. Being further pressed he exploded: 'Of course, if I were a woman, I'd simply refuse to speak to any man or do anything for man until I'd got the vote. I'd make my husband's life a burden, and everybody miserable generally. Women should have a revolution—they should shoot, kill, maim, destroy—until they are given the vote.'[5] In fact in a meeting of the National Union of Women's Suffrage Societies held on 26th March 1907 Shaw seconded a resolution that '... called upon the Government to introduce a bill conferring the franchise upon women.'[6] His speech on suffrage was also delivered there.

Yet Shaw was too wise to overestimate the importance of suffrage. He considered women's right to vote as a means of inducting them to public bodies. He knew no other effective way of making men behave properly without their presence on various committees. With this end in view, Shaw insisted on the inclusion of women on the managing committee of the Academy of Dramatic Art.

In his dramatic works also he attempted to propagate his special brand of feminism. In a burlesque called *Press Cutting* subtitled 'A Topical Sketch Compiled From the Editorial and Correspondence Columns of the Daily Newspapers During the Women's War of 1909.' Shaw treated the question of suffrage in his typical tongue-in-cheek style. His ambivalent attitude estranged many a feminist. But this controversial treatment of a serious issue is not new with Shaw who could proclaim himself an ardent champion of socialism yet reject the Marxist theory of surplus value. In *Major Barbara* he chose to solve the problems of poverty through the benevolent capitalism of 'money and gun power'. This shuttling between extreme seriousness and utmost levity is the essence of Shavianism, yet many of his admirers were baffled by it. In *Press cuttings* Shaw wanted to warn the over enthusiastic that women's suffrage was not a panacea. The women protagonists of this play wanted greater control through military power. The critics who laughed at his advanced idea of women's participation in Military service are now surprised to see his vision turn into a reality after a century. Moreover his main theme that suffrage was but a small step towards women's liberation has been admitted by most of the feminists of our own time.

In *The Fascinating Foundling* the heroine described the suffering of a suffragist on strike who has to eat at several restaurants on release. She defines marriage as an 'expensive and troublesome' institution. *Fanny's First Play* dealt with the suffragette movement more explicitly with its use of parellelism. In this play within a play with a suffragette in each, Shaw set the younger generation of educated girls against their old-fashioned parents. Fanny shocks the Count, her father, by writing a revolutionary play. Margaret, a 'springy girl of eighteen with 'a gaily resolute manner, even peremtory on occasions'[7] shocks her parents by her unabashed confession of having spent a fortnight in Holloway Gaol for assaulting a policeman. She speaks up for her sex as an exponent of the new morality: 'When I was at home and at school I was what you call good, but I wasn't free. And when I got free I was what most people call not good.'[8] Shaw's interest in and sympathy for the young rebellious generation of women accounts for the 600 performances the play had.

This struggle for freedom in defiance of conventional morality is the essential trait of the Shavian New Woman. She eschews the typical role of her sex because it interferes with her right to exist for herself. Margaret swaps her mother's image of herself as a 'heroine of romance' with her own self-image as 'heroine of reality.' She ruthlessly exposes her parents' effort to cover-up her stay in jail: 'That's all our respectability is pretending, pretending, pretending. Thank heaven, I have had it knocked out of me once for all.'[9]

In this knock-out between the conventional morality and the new morality it is the latter that wins. Margaret breaks off her engagement with a prig to marry the family valet. Both Fanny and Margaret represent the new emerging force that was to become a permanent feature of modern drama. The anti-romantic attitude which characterizes the Shavian heroine is used as a weapon to dismantle her stereotype role.

Shaw's ambivalence towards love and marriage is also revealed in his novels which were rejected by editors of London publishers for their too serious and unconventional tone. In *An Unsocial Socialist* (written in 1884), for example, Sidney Trefusis, Shaw's alter ego, runs away from the bondage of love and marriage because of the captivating beauty of the heroine. A phobia haunts him that the ensnaring power of love and sex will interfere with his work. So the *femme fatale* Henrietta is eventually replaced by his second wife Agatha Wylie who proves to be a worthy companion because she is not in love with him. The anti-romantic attitude is further carried on in *Love Among the Artist* (written in 1888). The hero-composer Jack is relieved at being rejected by the heroine because he believes that marriage would only ruin his creativity. Hence the novel ends with the disillusionment of an early cynic who concludes that it is better to starve the heart than overfeed it. Better still to feed it on fine food like music. Shaw's vulnerability to women's influence and his equal determination to extricate himself find expression in *Immaturity* (written in 1879). The hero's need for love and dedication to work conflict with each other. The problem is resolved by the intervention of the sublimation theory. There is no justification for marriage except for progeny and experiments in eugenics.

Shaw himself believed that *Irrational Knot* (written in 1887) was an attempt to write *A Doll's House* in English because of its morality—'original, not ready-made.' But ironically, the publishers were not convinced and returned the manuscript for its disagreeable characters and unconventional morality. It is worth noting that neither his early plays nor his novels were hailed by the Victorian public. The novels never saw the light of day; *Plays Pleasant and Unpleasant* (1898) were published and performed with the help of his own funds. Fifty or sixty rejection slips for his five novels without a single acceptance forced him to abandon novel writing.

Shaw's new morality was not of course quixotic. He came to believe in the economic basis of morality which is well-expressed in *Mrs Warren's Profession* and *Major Barbara* but the germination of this thought began with *The Irrational* Knot: 'Money is indeed the most important thing in the world; and all sound and successful personal and national morality should have this fact for its basis. Every teacher or twaddler who denies it or suppresses it, is an enemy of life. Money controls morality ....'[10] In a gesture of humility Shaw admitted that his novels were not readable enough to be recommended. But they are important for their autobiographical content and the evolution of Shavian philosophy. He was keen on proving that the 'new morality' or the revolt of the Life Force against the 'readymade morality' of the nineteenth century was not the work of a Norwegian microbe, but would have worked itself into expression in English literature had Norway never existed.[11]

Dominating women who became the hallmark of Shavian drama made their appearance in fiction much before they were inducted into his early plays. In the novels he shows more interest in female characters than the male. New women and new morality became permanent features of Shaw's works. His treatment of women was influenced by his early experience in social work. Lillah McCarthy narrated how Shaw was accustomed to co-operate with women in public work; and this enabled him to lift the relations of his men and women to a plane of equality unknown in the theatre.[12] His self-contradictory view of sex capable of 'producing celestial flood of emotion' and as something 'monstrous' and 'indecent' as spoken to Hesketh Pearson and G.K. Chesterton on different occasions is also present in his novels. The problem of sexuality became an undercurrent motif of all his works.

Shaw's major plays have little direct reference to the suffrage movement because he believed that women were competent enough to handle their own affairs, and men could not interfere 'without striking a false note, making a mess of it, and looking the most ignominious of captives.'[13] In truth Shaw was less interested in topical problems and more concerned with the eternal Woman Question. As a philosopher he realized that woman as a valuable human resource was shunted off the mainstream of life under false puritanism. His unwomanly woman was an attempt to counteract the damage done.

The Shavian heroine whom Shaw calls 'vital genius' is an enterprising woman with ideas of her own. Far from playing to the tune of other characters, she dominates them. The sheer force of her will power and unconventional character bewildered critics like Frank Harris who found her distinctly 'unpleasant, practically unsexed' and her 'pursuit has about as much sex appeal as a time table.' In *Themes in Drama* Ellen Gainer wrote about Shaw's 'dark and problematic view of sexuality' (Mentioned in YWES, Vol.72, p. 415). But only such androgynous women, Shaw believed, could bring change in the perception of society as to their true status. Shaw enunciated this view in *The Quintessence of Ibsenism*: 'The sum of the matter is that unless Woman repudiates her womanliness, her duty to her husband, to her children, to society, to the law, and everyone but herself, she cannot emancipate herself.'[14]

Shaw was never tired of repeating that a woman was a man in petticoats and vice-versa. But for the biological necessity which he called 'special occasion' and the business of reproduction, he wanted to obliterate the difference between the sexes and kept hoping that in the evolutionary process the sexual 'relationship' would be superseded by a spontaneous intellectual ecstasy in future. The romantic and the puritan clashed in him to produce an extreme view of sex.

Shaw's theory of the Superman is probably an attempt to sublimate the sexual energy of mankind which his puritan upbringing associated with a feeling of guilt. But this belief in the superman was a fad of the time under the influence of Bergson and Nietzsche, and to this he added his interest in eugenics. Shaw delegated this task of improving the human race to women whose instincts would guide them to select the right fathers for an improved race. Though the superman proved to be a fantasy, and eugenics earned a bad reputation because of its association with fascism, his creation of the new heroine, the vital genuis, became a new force in modern drama.

To make room for the New Woman Shaw set out to undermine the female archetype of the passive and docile woman yoked to household duties. The heroine of *The Fascinating Foundling* mocks the ideal of self-denial: 'you no doubt hold that self-sacrifice is a woman's chief amusement'[15] Shaw further argued in *The Quintessence of Ibsenism*:

> The domestic career is no more natural to all women than the military career is natural to all men; and although in population emergency it might become necessary for every able-bodied woman to risk her life in child-bed just as it might become necessary in a military emergency for every man to risk his life in the battlefield, yet even then it would by no means follow that the child-bearing would endow the mother with domestic aptitudes and capacities as it would endow her with milk.... If we have come to think that nursery and kitchen are the natural sphere of a woman, we have done so exactly as English children come to think that a cage is the natural sphere of a parrot: because they have never seen one any where else.'[16]

The old mindset had to go before his revolutionary ideas could be accepted by the common people. Shaw made fun of sanctity of marriage vows, a highly prized Victorian virtue, in *How He lied to Her Husband*, *The Philanderer* and *Arms and the Man*. Men insisted on this virtue to ensure their real successor in the family but women suffered because they could never prevent their men's affairs outside. Therefore Shaw treated it with levity as a virtue more extolled than practised. Even here men are more guilty than women. His anti-romanticism is deliberate and is consistent with his feminist outlook. Love and romance only chain women to their submissive role. In his usual hyperbolic style he satirized love, the staple food of commercial theatre and cinema. No man could, he argued, endure a total of ten minutes of love in his entire life. Shaw began his dramatic experiment with a romantic and passionate woman in *Widowers' Houses* and developed the anti-romantic intellectual heroine with *Mrs. Warren's Profession*. While he demystified romantic love, he never replaced it with philandering. 'Never make a hero of a philanderer.' he warned all.

The essence of Shavian art lies in his characterization. He not only delineated characters but saw the world from their point of view. Having conceived the characters first, he invented suitable plots which would convey his ideas. While drawing women he avoided the convention of making them more feminine and vulnerable than they deserved. The aggressive Shavian women would belong to the future and would replace the traditional romantic heroines worshipped on a pedestal and then relegated to the confinement of home and hearth. This explains why they discard their typical sexual role and behave as free agents like their male counterparts.

This shift of emphasis from man to woman protagonist is revealed in the choice of titles of his plays: *Mrs Warren's Profession*, *Candida*, *Major Babara*, *Fanny's First Play*, *The Fascinating Foundling*, *Saint Joan* and *The Millionairess*. In other plays like *The Philanderer*, *Captain Brassbound's Conversion*, *Getting Married* and *Misalliance*, the protagonists are all women though the titles do not necessarily bear their names.

In the elaborate stage directions Shaw provides detailed description of the women and their physical and mental characteristics to rule out ambiguity. The reiterative epithets are: 'robuster' 'energetic' 'well-built' 'well-fed,' 'strong-minded' and 'confident', 'terrifying' and 'formidable.' They speak volumes about the uniqueness of Shavian women and the new role they are destined to play. Surprisingly, Shaw's minor women characters and minor plays are rich in feminist ideas. Mrs Clandon of *You Never Can Tell* is introduced as 'a woman of cultivated interests rather than passionately developed personal affection.... She feels strongly about social questions and principles, not about persons.'[17] Such characterization drew the wrath of critics like Constance Barnicoate who found Shaw's women 'unlovable, unpleasing; they are either hard as nails like Vivie or merely bleating old sheep like Mrs Whitefield.' She was indignant at his inability to portray a genuine lady.[18] Surely Shaw's idea of a lady was farthest from the conventional notion.

The aggressive behaviour and unladylike speeches of the Shavian heroines are deliberate; Mrs Clandon makes a confession to her daughter's fiancé: 'Mr Valentine; you must excuse us all. Women have to unlearn the false good manners of their slavery before they acquire the genuine good manners of their freedom. Don't think Gloria vulgar: she is not really so.'[19]

The quality of independent thinking or ratiocination made the Shavian woman a class apart. The late Victorian and Edwardian societies were not yet ready for the new moral codes of the emancipated woman. She had to struggle against forces which wanted to keep her tied to her old role but she emerges as unrepentant and triumphant. Shaw, who described himself as 'a first-class ladies tailor' charted new paths for the New Woman. She is a woman of action and a reformer, a feminist, an intellectual and a philosopher—but above all she exists for herself as well as her sex. Grace Tranfield airs this new philosophy in *The Philanderer*: 'No Woman is the property of a man. A woman belongs to herself and to nobody else.'[20]

The creation of larger-than-life female characters is likely to be interpreted as the fantasy of a repressed male artist. Hence Clare Booth argued that Aristophanes and Euripides created magnificent women because they were woman-haters. As to Shaw she said that he could not handle women off-stage. He was afraid of them off-stage because he knew how strong women were. So he drew great female characters. On stage the play-wright could cope with them.[21] In a similar vein Virginia Woolf points out in *A Room of One's Own* how 'women in fiction' such as Cleopatra, Rosalind, the Duchess of Malfi, Millamant, Clarissa, Emma Bovary, Anna Karenina burnt like beacons, but in history she was locked up, beaten and flung about the room. She drives home the shocking truth most trenchantly: 'Imaginatively she is of the highest importance; practically she is completely insignificant. She pervades poetry from cover to cover. She is all but absent from history.'[22]

Distinguished biographers like Michael Holroyd, Hesketh Pearson and St. John Ervine provide us with abundant material about Shaw's married life as well as his extra-marital adventures with the New Women. As Shaw's public life was a whirlpool of controversies, so was his private life. There are two conflicting images of Shaw: a saint and an Irish Don Juan. His sexual life was torn between the longing of an amorous man for intimacy with beautiful women and his puritanical disgust with the sexual act. This dichotomy finds expression in his wishful thinking that the celestial flood of emotion and exaltation of existence felt during sexual intercourse will be superseded by intellectual ecstasy in future. Shavian heroines are the product of a highly imaginative mind perpetually attracted to the beauty and charm of strong women, but unable to cope with their possessiveness. This ambivalent attitude was fostered by his unhappy experience of first courtship of Alice Lockett. Shaw met her in 1881 when he was an impressionable and passionate youth and instantly fell in love. As a student of a vocal course conducted by his mother she felt a romantic fascination for Shaw but at the same time disliked the unsuccessful bohemian. Their growing incompatibility finally ended in estrangement. After her marriage with Dr. William Salisbury, a house surgeon, they remained barely friendly. To Shaw, Alice has a dual personality: as Miss Lockett she was ambitious and scornful; as Alice she was sympathetic and innocent. He tried in vain to rescue Alice from the grip of Miss Lockett. In his letters he summed up his impressions which kept haunting him during his preoccupation with political economy: '... any other man's heart would have stopped, but it put me in *suspense*, which is the essence of woman's power over man.'[23] In another letter he further confessed: 'I do not like myself, and sometimes I do not like you; but there are moments when our two unfortunate souls seem to cling to the same spar in a gleam of sunshine...'[24]

The fascination and the disenchantment produced in Shaw a curious combination of an incorrigible romantic obsession with strong women and an anti-romantic spirit as a neutralizing force. As a boy he loved and admired his mother, a professional musician, but was deprived of the care and attention he yearned for. The genesis of his ambivalence toward women in the Mother figures in his plays like Mrs Britomart and Mrs Clandon, Lady Cicely and Candida owes its existence to the influence of his dominating mother.

The New Women of the stage like Ellen Terry, Mrs Patrick Campbell, Florence Farr, Janet Achurch and Alma Murray also inspired him to create challenging roles to exploit their acting talents. The romantic artist who wanted to be in love with such beautiful and intelligent actresses was at war with the objective theatre director. Shaw met Ellen Terry in 1890 after an extended epistolary romance that lasted five years. He wrote the leading role of Lady Cicely in *Captain Brassbound's Conversion* specifically for her which she accepted after initial reluctance.

For Ellen the meeting was an anticlimax. The real Shaw fell short of her expectation. The levity of his manners seemed less admirable that the levity of his plays. The experience of his earlier unsuccessful affairs taught Shaw about the disenchanting effect of daily proximity. On 10 October, 1896, he wrote to her: 'I vow that I will try hard not to spoil my high regard, my worthy respects my deep tenderness, by any of those philandering follies which make me so ridiculous, so troublesome, so vulgar with women. I swear it. Only do as you have hitherto done with so wise an instinct: keep out of my reach.'[25]

Though he maintained a distance and insisted on her clothing herself 'in that most blessed of all things—unsatisfied desire,'[26] a deep longing for her love always persisted. A similar ambivalence is noticed in his courtship of Annie Besant. Shaw misled this strong woman into believing that he was 'a loafer.' She was reported to have drawn up an elaborate marriage contract of stringent terms and conditions which he declined as too exacting for his creative spirit. She felt somewhat let down when she later discovered the truth. Shaw created the stage character of Raina in *Arms and the Man* based on Annie Besant. He dramatised his impressions of two other powerful women in *The Philanderer*. His turbulent relationship with Jenny Patterson came to an end when she attacked and abused Florence Farr on 27 April 1891. He assured Florence Farr that Jenny could not shake the foundation of their relationship but it ironically turned out to be a move from the frying pan into the fire. The impressionable artist was once again upset by the possessiveness of Florence Farr. The relationship soured and he was driven to desperation in the letter dated 12.10.1896: '... now to be with you is hell: you make me frightfully unhappy.' He described their relationship as 'The relation of the North pole to the south'. Shaw had great regards for Florence Farr as an intelligent and honourable woman of business but had reservations about her acting talent.'[27]

Shaw's letter of 10 October, 1896 to Ellen gives insight into his ambivalence towards women of close acquaintance: 'It is only when I am being used that I can feel my own existence, enjoy my own life. All my love affairs end tragically because the women can't use me. They lie low and let me imagine things about them; but in the end a frightful unhappiness, an unspeakable weariness comes; and the wandering Jew must go in search of someone who can use him to the utmost of his capacity.'[28]

The longing to be used by his women rather than using them for his career was a typical Shavian attitude. The hyper-sensitive genius experienced similar turmoil in his relationship with Mrs. Patrick Campbell. In 'Saturday Review' dated 28.9.95. Shaw reviewed her performance as Juliet. While he praised her dance as 'irresistible' and 'immemorable,' her acting seemed 'immature.' However, he became interested in enlisting her after viewing her role as Rat wife in *Little Eyolf* in 1896. In his first encounter Shaw attempted to interest Mrs. Campbell in *The Devil's Disciple* by reading it to her. He wrote the part of Cleopatra for her in *Ceasar and Cleopatra*, a play that dramatised their relationship as critic and actress. He wanted her as Mrs Warren in *Mrs Warren's Profession*, as Julia in *The Philanderer*, and finally wrote the challenging part of the flower girl in *Pygmalion* specifically for her. She invited Shaw for business talks and accepted his offer. An intimate relationship with her rejuvenated Shaw at 56. In Mrs Pat. Shaw seems to have discovered what he had sought in Alice, Jenny Patterson, Florence Farr, and Charlotte. But tension built up when Mrs Pat wanted the status of wife and wished to bear his child. Finally she broke away with Shaw to marry George Cornwallis-West. Shaw's main problem was that he was inexorably fascinated by strong women and depended heavily on them for inspiration but the romance came to an end when their possessiveness interfered with his freedom. In his drama he created strong, intelligent and charming women without possessiveness.

Another interesting young woman Janet Achurch impressed Shaw at the *Doll's House* celebration dinner. He selected her for the role of Candida and made frantic attempts to save her from the menace of drug addiction. She on her part gave her best performance. Michael Holroyd offers his psychoanalytic view: In his relationship with women Shaw sought the attention and love denied by his mother. Sexual excitement produced in him ejaculation of words in the form of letters, novels and plays.'[29] Holroyd further explored why Shaw chose women as vehicles for his ideas: 'His Dublin home had been ruled by Licinda Elizabeth, not George Carr Shaw, and this he believed, was how the adult world was administered. Though the reconaissance work towards social change was done by men, society changed only when women wanted it to do so. Revolution came from men, evolution through women.'[30]

But Shavian feminism cannot be explained away as merely a product of a matriarchal family: it is a complex phenomenon. The prime motivation was to replace the outdated conventions of Victorian society with a new morality of his own. Like Victorian Capitalism, Shaw denigrated Victorian sexuality. The Victorian woman, he argued, was a masterpiece in sex appeal from the top of her head to sole of her feet. Her clothing was designed to emphasize her sexuality. The flowing and cumbersome clothes with their 'naughty little revelation of some kind'[31] intensified the sex appeal.

Shaw set out to correct the imbalance by taking off the cultural clothes which had stunted her personality. The task of undermining feminine sexuality and vesting women with a new androgynous role was a formidable one; nevertheless Shaw was successful as a trend-setter. Beatrice Webb interpreted Shaw's philandering as an ingenious way of getting materials for his plays. But Shaw the lover cannot be equated with Shaw the artist. The essence of Shavian feminism is women's right to equality and their emancipation from sexual role. His portrayal of women is more consistent with his theory than his personal experience with them. In the article entitled *Torture by Forcible Feeding is Illegal* published in the *New Statesman* dated 12 April, 1913, Shaw wrote: 'I myself have the rather original view about woman that she is very much the some sort of person as I am myself.'

This androgynous view is well-embodied in all his leading women characters like Vivie Warren, Barbara, Gloria and Lady Cicely. Some heroines like Blanche, Raina and Grace start with romantic interest but finally emerge as mature individuals who assert their rights with the male characters. A close examination of his plays reveals that the New Woman in her new role is a vision, not a fantasy which is unsystematic and uncontrolled imagination. She is born of a philosophy that without her desexualization the world could not be improved. The undercurrent of this new approach to female sexuality is consistently present in all his works. Like Foucault, Shaw also understood how sexuality assumed social control and power over life. The sex instinct was not a mere biological force but is overlaid with power relations. Moreover, Shaw was modest enough to disclaim credit for his achievement. In his Epistle Dedicatory to *Man and Superman* he writes: 'I find in my own plays that woman projecting herself dramatically by my hands (a process over which I assure you I have no more control than I have over my wife) behaves just as Woman did in the plays of Shakespeare.'[32]

Now the vexed question whether Shaw was a feminist is best assumed in the light of modern feminist theory. In *What is Feminism*? Rosalind Delmer defines a feminist as: '....someone who holds that women suffer discrimination because of their sex; that they have specific needs which remain negated and unsatisfied, and that satisfaction of these needs would require a radical change (some would say a revolution even) in the social, economic and politcal order.'[33]

Shaw definitely shared this broad view of feminism which aims at improving women's status in society; but he was also aware that feminism is a way of thinking created by, for and, on behalf of women—as something gender-specific. Like his special brand of realism and socialism, his feminism was also unique. Shaw substituted the concept of woman as a delicate and dependent creature with intelligent and active women. However, not all critics have paid glowing tributes to Shavian women. Sonja Lorichs in her thesis *The Unwomanly Woman in Bernard Shaw's Drama* complimented Shaw for his delineation of an entirely new type of woman and '... his sincere sympathy for and interest in women, his susceptibility to the discrimination of the sex and his never-failing promptitude to be their spokesman.'[34] Other critics however, think his plays are concerned with propagation of ideas, not with men and women of flesh and blood. A similar unfavourable view is also taken by Elsie Adams in 'Feminism and Female Stereotypes in Shaw' which set to deconstruct the 'critical cliche' that Bernard Shaw is the creator of startingly original fictional women'. Starting with a grudging acknowledgement that Shaw portrays 'arresting and powerful women' she maintains that. 'in spite of his departure from the nineteenth-century stereo-type of the demure, fragile "womanly" woman, he more often than not creates women characters who belong to types familiar in Western Literature. In play after play he presents us with various combinations of the traditional figure of temptress, goddess, or mother (usually with a capital M); and even when he creates a woman who had broken out of a traditional "female" role, he tends to draw another literary type—the "emancipated" woman.'[35]

She is equally emphatic in her concusion that the types do appear, however, and suggests the need to re-examine all Shaw's female characters. And as a starting point, '....we should stop exclaimining about their originality and make a clear distinction between Shaw's traditional treatment of women in the plays and his feminist politics.'[36] A great drama critic Eric Bentley said in an interview dated 14.10.85 that though female characters became symbols of freedom in Shaw's hands his feminism was much less modern. His condescending attitude is revealed in the title of *The Intelligent Woman's Guide to Socialism*.[37]

Jill Davis, while discussing the connections between late-ninteenth century socialism and emergent feminism takes Shaw to task for his own gender insecurity so that his 'new women' are ultimately as caricatured as those of Grundy.'[38] A positive view is however taken by Barbara Bellow Watson who made a systematic study of Shaw's women characters in *A Shavian Guide to Intelligent Women*. She says:

> 'Gathering up all that was implicit on the time, notably in the work of Ibsen, Shaw made explicit in his theories and vivid is his fiction, the 'new' assertion about women: that they exist as individuals quite apart from their sexual role. Even this however, fails to do justice to Shaw's assertion unless we add that his women can be characters and also heroines that in their eccentricity and egotism they are neither ridiculous nor horrible, but

charming and triumphant. Further they have a genuine importance as a protagonists.'[39]

She complimented and welcomed the Shavian women: 'Such is this heroine of Shaw's, who knows her own mind, speaks and acts her own mind, and in all the exuberance of her selfish vitality is irresistibly attractive to men.'[40] She congratulated Shaw for his original creation—'No, it is not Shaw's weakness that has invented this kind of woman, but his strength.[41]

Shaw's understanding of woman and the portrayal of her assertive character is possibly his greatest achievement which is only matched by his unusual wit and humour. His modest claim of being 'a first class ladies tailor' is true in the sense of that she is given an active role which is unprecedented. In contrast neither his superman nor New Man ever succeeded. Though Shaw did not invent the New Woman, he was responsible for her induction into the drama. Tennyson had predicted the emergence of the New Woman in 'The Princess: A medley' (1847) a poem written when the idea of a Woman's college was conceived by him:

> 'Oh I wish that I were some great princess, I would build
> Far off from man a college like man's
> And I would teach them all that men are taught:
> We are twice as quick.'[42]

As envisaged women's education contributed much to the struggle for their political as well as economic emancipation. As a visionary Shaw refused to overestimate the importance of women's franchise as realized by the later feminists. He raised vital issues of women's life in the plays and chose to solve their eternal problems with a new approach and a new morality. The new types of women he inducted into the plays become a new trend in drama.

II

Compared to the repressed heroines of Pinero and Jones, Shavian women came a long way towards their liberation. His heroines were cerebral women. They were iconoclasts and instruments of social transformation. The attack on Victorianism was a formidable task. Nevertheless, Shaw set himself to it with boundless energy in the very first play *Widowers' Houses* which struck the keynote of the new heroine. Blanche Sartorius is introduced as 'the strong-minded woman, presently lady-like' and is given a free rein to develop in diverse ways. This passionate and attractive woman dominates the play and its hero, Harry Trench. She belongs to the gallery of celebrated women characters which we may consider to be one of Shaw's greatest achievements.

Apart from the obvious socialist criticism of slum-landlordism, *Widowers' Houses* explore rather early what was to become a recurrent theme of his plays—the economic independence of woman and its corollary: her growth as an individual. In making love and breaking it she retains the initiative. But the strength of her personality comes from her education as well as financial security provided by her father. This financial self-reliance lays the foundation of a marriage based on equality. The wealthy father insists on giving his daughter a generous dowry to ensure her equal status in Trench's family, and Blanche is equally too proud to owe him anything. She will marry only on the condition of contributing equal income.

Blanche enjoys not only economic independence, she is also privileged to make decisions about her own life. When she breaks off the match with Harry for his reluctance to accept the tainted dowry, her father concedes to her wilfulness. But the idealist succumbs to her influence and finally sheds his idealism for commercial gain. Her exclamation about the hero seems more generic than particular: 'Well, let me tell you that you cut a poor figure, a very very poor figure, Harry.[43] Most of the male characters, like Harry, are eclipsed by the brilliant women in Shavian drama. A diminution of the hero's status is clearly visible and gradually the heroine seizes supremacy and wins him over to her pragmatic viewpoint. The relationship between the sexes assumes a new dimension, and the balance is clearly tilted in favour of women hitherto neglected to the point of oblivion. Shaw's first New Woman is 'fresh and attractive' and deliberately 'vital and energetic rather than delicate and refined.' Shaw's pet technique of reversal of the conventional theme—throwing away of the tainted gold into the Rhine—has been achieved through Blanche who induces Trench to give up his pseudo-idealism and participate in a profitable venture.

The Shavian New Woman grows maturer with every play till she culminates in the Superwoman—Lady Cicely. The heroine of *Mrs Warren's Profession*—Vivie Warren is a complete woman with a successful career and income of her own. Unlike Blanche she rejects her financial sponsor-parent because of the tainted source of income which conflicts with her ideology. Like Blanche she struggles for economic equality and individual freedom, but she shares none of her romantic passion. Her anti-romantic temperament and dedication to work is matched only by Lina Szczepanowska of *Misalliance*. In strength of character and single-minded pursuit of their goals, Vivie and Lina are in sharp contrast to the weak hero of *Widowers' Houses* who fails to live up to his ideal.

The New Woman's pursuit of psychological freedom is the theme of Shaw's second play, *The Philanderer*. In this extremely advanced comedy the heroine, Grace Tranfield breaks away from the ideals of the 'womanly woman' and proves herself to be a New Woman committed to self-reliance and self-respect. Shaw indicated the winds of change when he said 'Grace Tranfield, not Charteris is the hero of the play'. The word 'hero' is worth noting. It tells us about the transformation that was taking place in women's status. Before Shaw no other English dramatist ventured to give the central role to a woman. He is the first conscious and intrepid exponent of the woman question and directs his polemics to the various issues. This liberated widow with 'plenty of determination and self-respect' understands sexual politics too well to accept her lover's marriage proposal. She gives him up not only for his perpetual philandering but because of an apprehension of bondage which she articulates in no uncertain terms: '.... I will never marry a man I love too much. It would give him a terrible advantage over me: I should be utterly in his power. Thats what the New Woman is like.'[44]

Grace is one of the finest specimens of Shaw's New Woman endowed with 'sincere tenderness and dignified quietness.' Her poise and self-restraint are in sharp contrast with Julia, the excitable and sentimental 'womanly woman'. Her confession as an unsuccessful rival at the end of the play about her worthlessness symolizes the displacement of the 'womanly' heroine from the stage. The contemporary craze of the intelligentsia for Ibsen gave Shaw an opportunity to create a female protagonist with a new set of values. Grace 'can do without his love but not his respect.'[45] Ironically, the philanderer hero who maneouvers other characters to break off his relationship with Julia is eventually deserted by all. Shaw has sublimated the conventional theme of the duel of the sexes into the triumph of the new morality represented by the New Woman. True to her moral principle Grace remains resolutely independent even at the cost of loneliness. Her greatest contribution is her identification with her sex which finds expression in her satirical speeches: '... these our lords and masters' and 'No woman is the property of a man.'[46]

The quest for liberation begun by Blanche and Grace develops further in the career women like Vivie Warren and Lina Szczepanowska. The short-tempered passionate New Woman developes into a self-possessed, confident and sensible woman. At Beatrice Webb's suggestion Shaw created in Vivie Warren a real modern lady of the governing class who, brought up within a corrupt system, has the moral stamina, unlike Harry Trench, to reject it. The apparent protagonist Mrs. Warren, pressed by need, begins her crusade against capitalist exploitation only to perpetuate its vice. But her daughter Vivie parts company with her to retain her moral integrity. The independence of Vivie's character is based on the solid rock of economic independence and moral conviction. Vivie surpasses her mother not only in intelligence and education but also in a clear grasp of the central problem of their troubled relationship. She can sympathize with her mother as a victim of capitalism but turns her back on her when she chooses to continue her lucrative brothels for easy profits. To her Mrs. Warren is not so much guilty of immorality as of leading a life without conviction. Shaw intended Vivie to be a strong, self-confident career woman who could survive in a male-dominated profession of actuarial calculations and conveyancing. She wages a war against her mother's conventional values on the one hand and the romantic overtures of her lover Frank and the corrupt Crofts, the affluent business partner of Mrs Warren on the other. She rejects her mother's authority as vehemently as she avoids the trap of romance and marriage. She sums up her view of life in unambiguous terms: You (Mrs. Warren) want a daughter and Frank wants a wife. I don't want a mother; and I don't want a husband.'[47] She cures Frank of his 'love's young dream' with an emphatic snub: '... I must be treated as a woman of business, permanently single and permanently unromantic.'[48] A no-nonsense and unromantic attitude is the hall-mark of the Shavian woman. Vivie's final parting with her mother is symbolic of the New heroine severing her ties with the female archetype as well. Vivie proclaims: 'From this time I go my own way in my own business and among my friends. And you will go yours. Goodbye.'[49] This break with the past and creation of women with identities is a greater achievement for Shaw than his obvious attempt to draw 'attention to the truth that prostitution is caused, not by female depravity and male licentiousness, but simply by underpaying, undervaluing, and overworking women so shamefully that the poorest of them are forced to resort to prostitution to keep body and soul together.'[50] In his postscripts to the preface of 1933 edition of the play Shaw acknowledged with regret that the economic root of this evil was ruthlessly ignored by the profiteering press.

As the play progresses Vivie, with little resource except her education and ability completely dominates the woman of enormous wealth and social clout. In a war of nerves the mother represents the decadent 'Crofts philosophy of life' and the daughter the new outlook and new morality. Vivie's decision to remain permanently single for self-unfoldment is a new trend in modern drama to be followed by Lina, Lesbia and Lady Cicely. A heroine as a workaholic with no time either for romance or family is a new phenomenon on the dramatic horizon. Her relentless pursuit of freedom and physical strength overawe the good-for-nothing lover so much that he resigns himself to the role of her 'infatuated little boy.' The wily Crofts who tries to blackmail her into marriage is sized up and shown the door. She shows the unusual temerity of an advanced woman when she stands by her mother who fails to name her father. But she leaves her with fiery speeches because she represents a corrupt system: '....you are a conventional woman at heart. That is why I am bidding you good bye now'[51] and the New Woman's parting with the old woman is irrevocable: 'My work is not your work, and my way is not your way. We must part.'[52]

The female hero who made her debut in *Widowers' Houses* as a half-romantic, half-arrogant girl matured into a gracious lady in *The Philanderer* who renounced her lover to retain her independence. In *Mrs. Warren's Profession* Vivie's declaration about herself as 'permanently single and permanently unromantic' anticipates the assertive, feminism of the 1970s. The female hero reigns supreme in most of the early and middle plays of Shaw, particularly in some minor plays. And these new roles were performed by powerful actresses of the stage like Florence Farr, Mrs. Patrick Campbell, Alma Murray and Ellen Terry. The supremacy of women and their problems are carried on in *You Never Can Tell*, *Getting Married* and *Misalliance* with more gusto.

In *You Never Can Tell* the focus shifts from the conventional comic theme of a family quarrel and reconciliation to the duel of the sexes. But unlike Vivie and Mrs. Warren, the New Women, Mrs Clandon and Gloria Clandon fight their battle as a team against the tyrannical patriarch Crampton. The philandering hero Valentine resembles Charteris but is finally tamed to a settled life under the influence of the powerful Gloria. The duellists of sex, Crampton and Valentine accept graceful defeat at the hands of the feminist mother and her 'much more formidable daughter.'[53] Shaw has portrayed Mrs. Clandon as 'a woman of cultivated interests rather than passionately developed personal affections.'[54] In her youth she insisted on a married woman's right to own her property and championed the revolutionary ideas of Darwin, John Stuart Mill, Huxley, Tyndall and George Eliot. She struggled for the granting of University degrees, opening up professions and franchise to women. This unromantic woman who abhors display of personal sentiments and 'feels strongly about social questions and principles, not about persons'[55] is a successful innovation on the stage. Her commitment to feminism is evident from her grooming of Gloria to carry on her work. She is strong enough to raise her three children singlehandedly after her separation from her husband Mr. Cramption, an egoistic bully. When he returns after eighteen years to claim custody of his children he is humbled by the spirited wife.

The frivolous hero is so overwhelmed by Gloria's personality that he prefers to worship rather than marry her. And his avoidance of marriage on the pretext of financial insufficiency is overruled by her. Gloria handles her irresponsible father with a cool detachment and firmness reminiscent of her mother. She obeys only what is right and turns down Valentine's first proposal on the ground that the prevailing conditions of marriage are unacceptable to any self-respecting woman. This awareness of social and woman questions is the hallmark of the Shavian heroine. The enthralled hero admits being mentally and physically invigorated by the heroine's presence. Shaw knew only too well the importance of love scenes for theatrical success; but as his puritanical upbringing would not approve of sexual relationship as natural and healthy, he subconsciously developed the theory of creative evolution and eugenics to justify sexual union. After much ado about Valentine's kissing of Gloria, the tables are turned against male chauvinism and the duel of the sexes is eventually won by the heroine, whom Shaw calls the 'Twenteith Century woman.' The feminist mother and her enterprising daughter work as a team to fight patriarchal forces. All the sophisticated techniques of Valentine fall flat before her. The child of a broken marriage, Gloria develops an ambivalent relationship with Valentine for his 'lightness of head, lightness of faith and lightness of every thing' and sets out to reform his character. In this modern comedy of manners, women do unlearn the false good manners of their slavery in order to acquire the genuine manners of their freedom. Shaw delineated the heroine as the incarnation of haughty high-mindedness raging with the impatience of a mettlesome dominative character, who is summed up as 'a dangerous girl, one would say, if the 'moral passions were not also marked.' She is deliberately created to bring about a revolution on the stage. *You Never Can Tell* deals playfully with the taming of an egomaniac and a philanderer—a reversal of the theme of Shakespeare's *The Taming of the Shrew*. Male supremacy giving way to female domination became a reiterative feature of the Shavian play. Gloria considers herself a free woman and does not even allow her mother to encroach upon her right to make decisions about marriage.

Some of Shaw's minor plays like *Getting Married*, *Misalliance*, *Fanny's First Play* and *Press Cuttings* treat the woman question more dialectically. *Getting Married* subtitled 'A Disquisitory Play' and 'an instructive conversation' presents the complete woman who dispenses with the protection by male members. Lesbia, the self-confident, terrifying middle-aged lady prefers to embrace the life of a regular old maid for her principles of total independence and unconventional morality. Shaw was first to create intellectual heroines like Lesbia, Gloria and Lina who defy social conventions but are not sentimentally punished for their action.

These emotionally and intellectually mature women decide to substitute male companions with books and music. They are immune not only to love and romance but also to sexual appetite. Lesbia retorts to general Boxer that 'an English lady is not a slave to her appetites.'[56] Lina the Polish acrobat in *Misalliance* leaves the stuffy house in disgust because people there think of nothing but making love. She also criticises English society: 'your woman are kept idle and dressed up for no other purpose than to be made love to.'[57]

The most remarkable thing about Lesbia is that she develops her principles quite independently and refuses to compromise them either for financial security or biological necessity. She regards motherhood as a full-time job and demands to be paid for child-bearing. As a mother cannot properly bring up her children if she has to attend to her husband at the same time, she suggests the clearing out of men for two years from the house after each child birth. She spurns marriage because society would not allow such an arrangement. As an alternative to conventional marriages she suggests entering into an alliance with General Boxer. This idea of marriage by covenant or 'living together' was quite *avant garde* in Edwardian society. But while all other characters talk about the need for reform of marriage laws, Lesbia alone prefers her freedom to the comforts and security of marriage. 'There are certain rights I will not give any person over me.'[58] She asserts. As a pragmatist she sees men as they are and shows better understanding of the power game that is involved in sexual relationship. With incisive intellect she surpasses the bishop who is writing a book on the history of marriage and advocates making divorce reasonable and reform at the root. 'If you will only make marriage reasonable and decent, you can do as you like about divorce.'[59] Her self-imposed spinsterhood is a protest against male-biased marriage and divorce laws.

Another New Woman is Edith who publicly calls some politicians 'tyrants, liars, and thieves' and declines to marry after she hears from a pamphlet that a wife cannot divorce a criminal husband which she interprets as an inducement to wickedness. Like Lesbia, Edith also demands a remuneration for housekeeping and a thousand pounds for each child-bearing. Leo goes further and attacks the male monopoly of polygamy by reversing the roles: she proposes to keep her husband for everyday and her lover for concerts, theatres and going out in the evening. Rebellious women and their aggressive attitude were part of a Shavian game to rouse the soporific public about the woman question. It was a breakthrough for English drama when heroines came out of male hegemony to make decisions about their own lives. Even the age-old tradition of marriage is not too sacrosanct to be spared their ratiocination and revaluation.

In the preface Shaw explored the roots of women's bondage and blamed the male-biased marriage laws. Far from liberating women politically and personally, the laws reinforce their bondage. He attacked the tenth commandment which classified woman with a man's ox and his ass; this culture treated male adultery with indulgence and frowned upon female adultery as wicked. Shaw wanted to do away with the concept of women as property and asserted: 'the attack on marriage is an attack on property.'[60] What retarded the social progress of women was their economic dependence. He deplored the indignity of husband-hunting by the marriageable daughters of a poor family and held that a decent family life was impossible without raising their economic status. Marriage was not romantic; it was economic slavery. To him there was no more difference between marriage and prostitution than there was between Trade unionism and unorganized labour. He clinched his argument with sarcasm: '... as the economic dependence of women makes marriage a money bargain in which the man is the purchaser and the woman the purchased, there is no essential difference between a married woman and the woman of the street.'[61] A cynical view, but hard to refute. Shaw predicted that conventional marriage as an institution would cease to exist if woman had an alternative to the economic slavery and divorce were as easy as dissolution of a business partnership.

Shaw drew attention to the deep-seated sense of property in Antony's remark on Cleopatra: '... found you as a morsel' (*Antony and Cleopatra*, III.3.116) and Othello's '... keep a corner in the thing I love for others' uses' (*Othello*, III.3.272). His *avant garde* idea of open marriage received a jolt when a lady remarked with disgust that she would sooner lend her toothbrush than lend her husband to another woman.

To achieve economic independence women needed a new outlook and a new morality. In the preface to *Getting Married* Shaw deconstructed the romantic view of love and marriage; in the play he created women who spurn marriage as stupid and slavish. Though love and romance dominated the stage and literature, he reminded us, in real life it occupied 'a very small fraction indeed of time. The romance after marriage was even less.' He added: 'The majority of married couples never get to know one another at all; they only get accustomed to having the same house, the same children and the same income, which is quite a different matter.'[62]

The anti-romantic attitude in Shaw's case was not an expression of cynicism; it was an effective weapon to destroy the hypocritical morality which led women back to slavery. He advocated women's right to become mother 'without the obligation to become the servant of a man.'[63] He also recommended dissociation of sexual experience from marriage, and proclaimed it to be a cornerstone of all political constitutions. Shaw wanted young men not to have any illusion about sex and love and advised them to look upon love as an appetite which loses much of its attractions through gratification and 'no profession, promise or proposal made under its influence should bind anybody.'[64]

From marital bondage Shaw shifted his attention to parental interference in *Misalliance* subtitled 'A Debate in One Sitting". In his effort to highlight the communication gap between children and their parents, Shaw creates an angry woman Hypatia, who loathes home, parents, family, duty and respectability. This unconventional English girl 'of boundless energy and audacity held in leash' avoids the misalliance with Bentley, 'a member of the great and good middle-class.'[65] She prefers the mature and experienced Lord Summerheys but she finally settles with the young and intelligent Percival. Endowed with an instinctive understanding of sexual politics, she resolves to marry some one in love with her rather than marry the person she loves. Her new outlook and bold rejection of the old morality is clearly expressed. '...I don't want to be good; and I don't want to be bad. I just don't want to be bothered about either good or bad. I want to be an active verb.'[66]

Woman as a doer is a new Shavian concept. Hypatia fights against parental encroachment disguised as protection. She asserts: 'I'll not have my affairs interfered with by men on pretence of protecting me. I am not your baby.'[67]

The subtle understanding of male hegemony makes her immune to it. Shaw inducted a Polish woman to highlight the impassable eternal gulf between parents and children. The polish acrobat Lina Szczepanowska is determined to carry on her family tradition of daily adventure. This 'man-woman or woman-man' with a predilection for risky occupation and an unromantic disposition seizes the central role after crashlanding her aeroplane. She overpowers an intruder by her physical strength and later invites him to her gymnasium to make a man of him. She cures old Tartleton's infatuation by flatly rejecting his proposal and advising him to take physical exercises. Lina fulfills Shaw's concept of the complete woman. Unlike Hypatia she fights for her sex which is evident from her parting feminist speech. A serious preoccupation of Shaw was to liberate women from their romantic role which was detrimental to their economic independence. Lina is a brilliant case in point. Tartleton subjected the sexual role to polemical analysis. 'Why opposite (sex)? We are all human males and females of the same species. When the dress is the same, the distinction vanishes.'[68]

However, the distinction was not easy to obliterate. The success of Shavian woman was a positive step towards changing the mindset of the theatre-goers. Woman's struggle for a better social status is also evident in *Pygmalion* (1912). Though belonging to the lower class Eliza shows enough tact and tolerance to pursue her self-improvement but asserts herself when her overbearing mentor hurts her dignity. Her liberation begins with education under a typical patriarch but she soon outgrows his expectations and prepares herself for an independent career. The conflict begins when Prof. Higgins loses interest in her as a person once his successful experiment is over. She protests being a mere guinea pig for his phonetic experiment and seeks autonomy: 'I should be independent of both you and father and all the world.'[69] Eliza's real transformations is the maturing of her personality—a fact which is even acknowledged by the peevish phonetician: 'Five minutes ago you were like a millstone round my neck. Now you're a tower of strength: a consort battleship.'[70]

The transformed Eliza is not of Prof Higgin's making. She is neither a guineapig at the mercy of her experimentor nor a Frankenstein's monster to overpower his master. She emerges as the New Woman with a capacity for independent thinking and endowed with the will power to carry out her convictions. When Prof Higgins inquired if Freddy could make anything of her by marrying her, she rightly pointed out that she did not share his thought of 'making anything of one another' which was unnatural. Rather than going back to the gutter, she decides to compete with her mentor in his own profession. More startling is her decision to swap sexual roles. Instead of being dependent on her husband's income Eliza offers to act as bread winner and provide for Freddy after marrying him. This trend in gender role reversal surfaced in *Misalliance* when Lina took charge of security of men and Lady Cicely commanded brigands and judges with a rare finesse in *Captain Brassbound's Conversion*. Much of Shaw's novelty's owed to this dramatic technique.

In *Captain Brassbound's Conversion* Lady Cicely dominates the situation by her commanding personality. Her understanding of the power-structured relationship between the sexes helps her achieve complete control over all the male characters. Except Saint Joan, no other heroine comes closer to the superwoman than Lady Cicely Waynflete. Her role was tailormade for the great Ellen Terry who, Shaw thought, was wasting her talents in costume plays. This highly intelligent, mature woman of cunning simplicity, great vitality and humanity dominates the entire play and may be regarded the female equivalent of Shaw's Ceasar, the Superman. With tact and sympathy she exerts enormous influence on men. Shaw described her as 'A woman of great vitality and humanity who begins a casual acquaintance at the point usually attained by English people after thirty years' acquaintance.'[71] By her moral and intellectual superiority she persuades Captain Brassbound to shun his scheme of violent revenge. Shaw was exceedingly happy to be able to create this fascinating woman without exploiting sexual interest. And he wanted to reform the theatre of his time with the same zeal Lady Cicely shows in the conversion of Brassbound.

Throughout the play Shaw has emphasized her qualities of leadership—a natural ruler of men with the authority of a mother. Confident and unorthodox she crossed Africa with a dog and handled strangers with the dexterity of a trained diplomat. She explains the secret of interpersonal skill: 'Why do people get killed by savages? Because instead of being polite to them, and saying How dye do? like me, people aim pistols at them. I have been among savages—cannibal and all sorts. Everybody said they'd kill me. But when I meet them, I said Howdyedo? And they were quite nice. The kings always wanted to marry me.'[72] Woman as leader is a Shavian innovation which adds a new dimension to drama. This humane lady not only tolerates the repulsive captain with good humour but tames him by sympathizing with his unhappy upbringing. Despite threats of 'the justice of vengeance' she undertakes her journey, takes great care of his escorts and with diplomatic charm supersedes the authority of the captain who is reduced to a hapless onlooker. In the face of abrupt threat of relentless revenge by the captain, Sir Howard is startled but Lady Cicely does not lose her poise.

The New Woman with her usual self-possession carries on her charitable work of nursing a wounded escort and mending Brassbound's coat even when Sir Howard is taken prisoner. Her remarkable courage is revealed not only in her crossing Africa with a dog and surviving among six cannibal chiefs, but also setting a high moral standard: a woman providing leadership to a mixed group of an English judge, a U.S. Navy Captain, the Muslim Sidi and the intractable African brigand. The impact of her superior intelligence is complete and all-pervasive.

She successfully persuades Brassbound to shun violence and hatred towards Sir Howard whom he thought 'a thief and a murderer.' She tames his wild instincts by comparing him with his equally vindictive uncle. Her cool reasoning helps Brassbound realise the futility of revenge as much as it prevents Sir Howard's attempt to indict Brassbound for his alleged threat to sell him into slavery. With great diplomacy she makes these two intractable opponents give up vindictiveness and see reason. The hostile Sidi Assif falls in love with her. Even Kearney, the righteous judge was won over by her insinuation about a scandal and the sentiments of his dead wife. While dissembling to let everybody have his will she ultimately has everybody under her firm control. At the trial under Captain Kearney she pretend to tell the exact truth but prevaricates unabashedly to have Brassbound exonerated. She commands the crew of the U.S. ship without consulting the captain and wins strangers to her side by the compliments about their face. Yet his intellectual woman is not without a human heart; she falters when Brassbound proposes to her. The real strength of her character is revealed when she declines the proposal of an emotionally dependent captain looking for a commander as wife.

The woman of action parts company with the "Idealist the Impossibilist' with an epiphany: 'I have never been in love with any real person; and I never shall. How could I manage people if I hadn't that mad little bit of self left in me? That's my secret.'[73] Her overpowering presence is best summed up by Sir Howard: 'Half a dozen of such women would make an end of law in England in six months.'[74]

According to the latest Shavian biographer, Michael Holroyd, Lady Cicely epitomizes Shaw's ideal woman. Shaw created the role of another powerful woman, an idealist, for Eleanor Robson. *Major Barbara* remained a controversial play because of its disillusionment with and ambivalence towards socialism and the final triumph of capitalist philanthropy. The onus of fighting the mighty capitalist do-gooder is placed on his daughter, Barbara, the committed social worker. The economic argument of Mr. Undershaft may at present appear more plausible in the wake of worldwide collapse of socialist governments, but his emphasis on salvation through 'money and gun power' and solving the problems of poverty by violent means will remain controversial. Beatrice Webb, Shaw's Fabian comrade and the intellectual and biographical model for Barbara criticized it as 'the triumph of the immoral purpose.' The conversion of the firebrand idealist Barbara at the end seems forced and unconvincing. Like saintly Lady Cicely Major Barbara dedicates herself to the service of the poor and the distressed; but she is more ardent and less tactful. The dramatic conflict is heightened by the resistance put up by this New Woman of intense vitality against the destructive forces of 'mutilation and murder.' Andrew Undershaft's fiery polemics of 'freedom and power' through 'money and gunpowder' pales before the spiritual faith and quiet dignity of Barbara. She is visibly disillusioned by the deceitful practice of accepting tainted donations from the wine and ammunition merchants but she never compromises with her ideal. In contrast, her fiancé, the professor of Greek is too easily won over by the millionaire tycoon to be the successor to the lucrative 'factory of death and devastation.' As a play it never succeeds because the Prince of Darkness is allowed to eclipse the innocence of his saintly daughter. Yet *Major Barbara* remains primarily a drama of Barbara's growth from naiveté to worldy wisdom and maturity through experience. It is about her conversion from ineffectual socialism to the omnipotent force of capitalism. Undershaft's theory of preaching religion to well-fed people is as commonplace as his violent method of abolishing poverty is outrageous: 'I hate poverty and slavery worse than any other crimes whatsoever. And let me tell you this. Poverty and slavery have stood up for centuries to your sermons and leading articles: they will not stand to my machine guns. Don't preach at them: don't reason with them. Kill them.'[75] Fortunately the world has not shown much enthusiasm for his Utopian capitalism and its bloody method.

The saving grace of the play is that only Lady Britomart, the estranged wife could see through such specious dialectics and dismiss this high philosophy as nonsense and 'abominable wickedness.' Written in 1907 Undershaft's belligerent ideas seem perverse after the two horrible World Wars. Lady Britomart had the courage to leave her millionaire husband for preaching immorality and single-handedly brought up her children. As a woman of principle she never compromised with him though his money and power had Europe under his thumb. She remains unruffled till the end and as an emancipated woman allows her children to choose their career. Barbara emerges a winner as she decides to continue her work of reforming the souls of 'fullfed, quarrelsome, snobbish, uppish creatures' of the cannon factory. With all his brilliance Undershaft proves himself an anti-hero. More unscrupulous is the ideological *volte face* of Prof. Cusins. In 1933 Shaw added a postscript to the preface to regret that his view of poverty as an infectious pestilence went unheeded. But what deserves special attention is the new phenomenon of the heroine as an idealist and the fact that the play is centred on her fate. Shaw has underplayed the feminine element in Barbara's role: unromantic, businesslike, she is truly androgynous in thoughts and actions.

A saintly woman of superior intelligence also dominates Shaw's *Androcles and the Lion* which he called 'A Fable Play.' The most eloquent exponent of philosophy and religion is Lavinia, a young resolute woman of higher social standing. At the end of the play she vindicates woman's supreme role as mother: only a courageous mother is capable of giving birth to brave children. This truth is vindicated by Betty Frieden's later works.

In *Major Barbara* Shaw denounced Victorian morality: 'Well, you have made for yourself something that you call a morality or a religion or what not. It doesn't fit the facts. Well, scrap it. Scrap it and get one that does fit. That is what is wrong with the world at present. It scraps its obsolete steam engines and dynamics; but it won't scrap its old prejudices and its old moralities and its old religions and its old political constitutions.'[76]

This new morality was embodied by Shavian woman: Lady Britomart and Mrs Clandon leave their immoral husbands, heroines like Vivi, Grace, Lesbia and Lady Cicely willingly embrace the freedom of unencumbered spinsterhood. Lina and Blanche show a positive attitude to money and career which shocked the puritan. *The Doctor's Dilemma* begins with the problem of choosing between the honest but mediocre Dr Blenkinsop and the dishonest artistic genius Dubedat for treatment of tuberculosis, but has further ramifications.

The artist with his bigamy and other financial sharp practices turns out to be more scrupulous than Dr. Ridgeon who allows him to die without medical treatment with the evil design of marrying his 'arrestingly good-looking' widow. Far from being flattered she shocks the 'little man who tried to kill a great one' by her outright rejection of the marriage proposal. Jennifer Dubedat proves herself a woman of substance to the murderer of her husband: 'You are clever enough to puzzle me, but not to shake me.' The fate of the renowned doctor is decided by the New Woman who dismisses him as 'an elderly man' and remarries another to fulfil her dead husband's wish. She also shows enterprise in organising a solo exhibition of Dubedat's paintings and publishes his biography posthumously. A new dimension is added to drama when women who had always been relegated to passive roles decide the outcome of the play.

Enterprise and initiative are also the hallmark of the protagonist of *Man and Superman*. Ann 'the vital genius' is committed to the improvement of the human race by creating the superman. The pursuit of the intellectual Tanner by the heroine is a reversal of the woman-on-the-pedestal theory. And Shaw was never tired of repeating that her concern for evolving a better race is not personal business but every woman's concern for the fate of the universe. In Shavian dialectics: (as expressed in the Epistle Dedicatory to Arthur)'... every woman is not Ann; but Ann is Every woman.'[77] To defend the vitality and initiative of Ann, Shaw referred to Shakespearean heroines; but intellectuals like Vivie, Grace, Lesbia and Lina are not known even in Shakespear's plays. After a century Shaw's philosophy of life force evokes little response but the idea of the woman as the chief instrument of social change is now too widely held to raise any eyebrow. Ann's influence on male characters is so profound that anti-feminist charges have been levelled against her. But the comic treatment of a serious theme sprinkled with Tanner's use of animal imagery—'the boa constrictor,' 'the bee,' 'the spider' points more to the hunting instincts of Life Force. The idea repelled Christopher Caudwell who took him to task for rewriting 'the history of reality in terms of witch-doctor's "life force" and neglecting science.'[78] Tanner, as spokesman of Shaw, shows a change in man's perception of woman's role when he admires Violet for conceiving without the solemnization of marriage: 'But I know and the whole world really knows though it dare not say so that you were right to follow your own instinct; that vitality and bravery are the greatest qualities a woman can have, and motherhood her solemn initiation into womanhood; that the fact of your not being legally married matters not one scrap, either to one's own worth or to our real regard for you.'[79] Shaw has advanced women's cause making them men's competitor and sometimes their superior. The conventional criticism of Ann as stereotype huntress is not fair: as Every woman she is in quest of a father for the Superman. Any personal ambition is ruled out in favour of genetic upgrade of the human race. What is noteworthy is the active role played by woman in contrast to her traditional passive role. But as she is engaged in husband-hunting, which is a stereotype feminine role, neither she nor the play quite succeeds.

In *Candida* Shaw presents a wife as the decision-maker. Having complete autonomy she manoeuvres her husband and the poet lover to a crisis where she must choose one and leave the other. In a similar situation in Ibsen's *The Lady from the Sea* the wife is cured of her obsession for a seafaring stranger only when her husband allows her a free choice. Shaw once again reversed the traditional roles of the sexes: the fate of a doll husband is decided by his dominating wife. In addition to the usual 'well-built,' 'well-nourished' features Shaw has emphasized her 'courageous eyes, and well-set mouth and chin[which] signify largeness of mind and dignity of character to ennoble her cunning in affections.' The husband, a first rate clergyman, robust and full of energy has been hailed as 'a great baby' for his vanity and self-complacency. The conventional theme of an incompatible marriage takes an unconventional turn when the wife, though in love with a young poet, decides to stay with her prosaic husband because he happens to be the weaker of the two and needs her care and attention more.

Candida has the power to control the fate of both. The clergyman is packed up for his scheduled lecture; the imaginative lover is made to lay the table. She treats both the boys and spurns the glowing attributes of 'goodness and purity' as 'nasty uncomfortable things'. Both men are unimpressive: Marchbanks could neither transcend his servility nor assert his right as a lover. Morell with his claim of being bigger and stronger is sized up by Candida as a boy who needs her constant protection. Her decision to stay with the husband is her free choice. The lover is dispensed with because he can do without happiness. Candida starts with the autonomy which is attained by Ellida at the climax of her struggle—certainly a leap forward but discounted by some critics as anti-feminist.

Shavian women come out of the cocoon of Victorian prudery and attain a new status in the theatre. The Woman no longer plays the passive role of the coy mistress and docile wife. As vital genius she plays multifarious roles: she creates a new image of an intelligent educated and assertive individual who pursues economic freedom for her self-development. She thinks, reasons and fights for equal status in a male-dominated culture. When thwarted, she is angry, defiant and recalcitrant, often unwomanly and unromantic. She emerges as an essentially political character. With resourcefulness and ingenuity she seizes the central role in almost all the plays. With rare courage and conviction she changes the concept of woman's role and ushers in a new trend which is carried on by other contemporary playwrights like Granville Barker and Galsworthy. Critics who explained the assertive Shavian woman in terms of the influence of his dominating mother missed the point. She is not merely a projection of repressed desire or a re-creation of the matriarchal culture of his childhood. She represents Shaw's vision of a world—equitable and androgynous—the right ambience for men and women to grow in and make this earth a habitable place for all.

NOTES AND REFERENCES

1. Jackson Russell, ed., *Plays By Henry Arthur Jones* (London, Cambridge U.P. 1982) p. 160.
2. George Rowell, ed., *Plays by A.W. Pinero*, (London, Cambridge, Un., 1986) p. 131.
3. Rodelle Weintraub, ed., *Fabian Feminist: Bernard Shaw*, (University Park, Pennsylvania Un., 1977) p. 11.
4. *Why All Women are Particularly Fitted to be Good Voters*, N. York, 21 April, 1907.
5. *Fabian Feminist*, p. 237.
6. H. Dan Laurence, ed., *Bernard Shaw: Collected Letters*, 1911-1925, (London, Max Reinhardt, 1985) p. 81.
7. Shaw: *Plays*, p. 666.
8. *Ibid.*, p. 667.
9. *Ibid.*
10. Shaw: *The Irrational Knot* (London, Archibald Constable, 1905) p. xiv.
11. *Ibid*, p. xxv.
12. Lilian McCarthy, *The Annual Journal of Bernard Shaw Studies*, Vol-3, p. 165.
13. Shaw: *Collected Letters*, 1911-25. p. 18.
14. Bernard Shaw, *The Quintessence of Ibsenism*, (London, Constable & Co, 1913) p. 41.
15. Shaw: *Play*, p. 1124.
16. *The Quintesseence of Ibsenism*, pp. 39-40.
17. Shaw: *Plays*, p. 176.
18. *Fortnighty Review*, March, 1906.
19. Shaw: *Plays*, p. 215.
20. Shaw: *Plays*, p. 30.
21. Weinrtraub, ed., *Fabian Feminist*, p. 212.
22. Alice S. Rossi, ed., *The Feminist Papers* (N. York, Columbia Un. Press, 1973) p. 637.
23. *Collected Letters*, Vol. 1. p. 64.
24. *Ibid.*, p. 112.
25. *Ibid.*, p. 677.
26. *Ibid.*, p. 702.

27. *Ibid.*, p. 686.
28. *Ibid.*, p. 676.
29. Michael Holroyd, *Bernard Shaw: 1856-1898: The Search for Love*, Vol-1, (London, Chatto & Windus, 1988) p. 108.
30. *Ibid.*
31. Shaw: *Platform and Pulpit*, p. 203.
32. *The Complete Prefaces of Bernard Shaw*, (London, Paul Hamlyn, 1965), p. 155. Henceforth it will be briefly referred to as: Shaw: *Prefaces*.
33. Juliet Mitchell and Ann Oakley, ed., *What is Feminism?* (London. Oxford Un. 1986) p. 3.
34. Sonja, Lorichs, *The Unwomanly Woman in Bernard Shaw's Drama.* (Uppasala, 1973) p. 13.
35. Weintraub, *Fabian Feminist*, p. 156.
36. *Ibid.*, p. 161.
37. *The Annual Shaw Studies*, Vol-7, pp. 10-11.
38. *Year's Work in English Studies*, vol-73,1992, p. 473 (Briefly known as YWES).
39. Barbara Bellow Watson, *A Shavian guide to Intelligent Woman*, (London, Chatto & Windus, 1964) p. 17.
40. *Ibid.*, p. 24.
41. *Ibid.*
42. Quoted by Josephine Johnson in *Florence Farr: Bernard Shaw's New Woman* (Gerrards Cross, Colin Smythe, 1975) p. 17.
43. Shaw: *Plays*, p. 27.
44. *Ibid.*, p. 46.
45. *Ibid.*, p. 52.
46. *Ibid.*, p. 30.
47. *Ibid.*, p. 91.
48. *Ibid.*, p. 87.
49. *Ibid.*, p. 89.
50. Shaw: *Prefaces*, p. 219.
51. Shaw: *Plays*, p. 92.
52. *Ibid.*, p. 91.
53. *Ibid.*, p. 176.

54. *Ibid.*
55. *Ibid.*
56. *Ibid.*, p. 177.
57. *Ibid.*, p. 551.
58. *Ibid.*, p. 642.
59. *Ibid.*, p. 573.
60. *Prefaces* (93 ed.) p. 413.
61. *Ibid.*, pp. 446-47.
62. *Ibid.*, p. 420.
63. *Ibid.*, p. 430.
64. *Ibid.*, p. 439.
65. Shaw: *Plays*, p. 611.
66. *Ibid.*, pp. 617-18.
67. *Ibid.*, p. 639.
68. *Ibid.*, p. 621.
69. *Ibid.*, p. 749.
70. *Ibid.*, p. 751.
71. *Ibid.*, p. 301.
72. *Ibid.*, p. 303-304.
73. *Ibid.*, p. 331.
74. *Ibid.*, p. 324.
75. *Ibid.*, p. 499.
76. *Ibid.*, p. 498.
77. *Prefaces* (65), p. 161.
78. Christopher Caudwell, *Studies & Furter Studies in a Dying Culture* (London, M.R., 1971) p. 3.
79. Shaw: *Plays*, p. 350.

GRANVILLE BARKER: NEW WOMAN AS MORAL GENIUS

4

As an able director and actor Granville Barker became a worthy exponent of the New Drama and the synergy of his collaboration with Shaw offered the audience drama of great merit. At a professional level they were both playwright and critic, and in personal life they were Fabians and collaborators who worked towards the creation of a new drama destined to displace the commercial theatre of the day. Endowed with impressionable and romantic temperaments, they depended heavily on women for their creativity. In both cases fathers played an insignificant role in early life; dominant mothers moulded their characters and careers. Their professional success owes much to of the New Women of the stage. In spite of the resemblance and the intellectual indebtedness, Granville Barker was too much of an individualist to be treated as either Shaw's shadow or his dramatic disciple.

As a propagandist, Shaw used his characters as brilliant exponents of his ideas, but Barker, essentially a director, created probable situations which enabled his characters to live the ideas. Their women characters are as different as their treatment of sexuality is varied. While Shavian women are the embodiment of energy and enterprise, Granville Barker's women are the 'epitome of all that aesthetic culture can do to a woman.'[1] The introvert women of his plays draw their inspiration from an inner spiritual strength, while Shavian women dominate the plays by virtue of their superior intellect and will-power. Their common trait is the courage to fight male oppression and social evils. In *The Marrying of Ann Leete* Granville Barker used the contemporary phrase 'The New

Woman' to describe Ann, the 'uncompromising young lady' of late eighteenth century. This anachronism confirms his concern for the women's position. The New Woman needs a 'new world' to expand her mental horizon. Unlike the typical timid woman of Victorian age, she can take 'big risks' which implies defying social conventions and facing social censure for one's personal convictions. In place of the intellectual dynamism of Shavian woman we have a woman who is 'well-balanced' and 'nearly always happy' and to crown her maturity she is endowed with a 'faith to go on.' This resilience makes them a class apart. Each woman fights against a powerful and deep-rooted tradition.

Shaw's acquaintance with Granville Barker began with the fruitful collaboration for the staging of *The Admirable Bashville* in 1903 at Court Theatre and further deepened with Granville Barker playing the parts of Marchbanks and Tanner. The friendship and intimacy fuelled the idle speculation that Granville Baker was Shaw's natural son. To Shaw, Barker as actor was less admirable than the author of *The Marrying of Anne Leete* which he regarded as the finest bit of literature and an exquisite play. In fact, Barker's reputation as a critic, director and actor obscured his contribution to modern drama. Of his seven plays only four—three comedies and a tragedy—are known to the public. Modern evaluation is slowly beginning to regard him as a major playwright of beauty and subtlety who probed the depths of the human soul. However, his treatment of sexuality and the portrayal of the new heroine have not been subjected to close scrutiny. Like his contemporaries, Barker believed in libido as the mainspring of most human activities, and also the root of nervous illness. He also seems to subscribe to the theory of sublimation of sexual energy.

Despite his protest, it is not unlikely for Granville Barker to be influenced by Shaw, eighteen of whose plays he directed for hundreds of performances. And like Shaw he believed that the living conditions of the masses must be improved before art and culture could flourish. Women's issues are his recurring themes because they are an integral part of social progress. The outstanding success of the new drama is a tribute to the new social consciousness. The Vadrenne-Barker management of Court Theatre gave 988 performances of thirty-two plays by seventeen playwrights during 1904-1907 out of which Shaw's eleven plays had 701 shows. Next to Shaw were Granville Barker with 34 shows and Galsworthy with 29 shows.

The subtle methods of Granville Barker stand out in sharp contrast to the intellectual bulldozing of Shaw. Barker's women characters start with the limitations of being feminine and come closer to average Victorian women whereas Shavian women are modelled on the dominating figures of the time. As a faithful portrayal of society Barker's plays are closer to reality than Shaw's. The superior capabilities and achievements of Shavian women are more of a vision of things-to-come at the expense of realism and this incurred the consternation of the feminists. The brilliant victories of Shavian women often seem less convincing than the quiet dignity and the spiritual convictions of Barker's heroines. Victorian double standards and sexual hypocrisy are ruthlessly exposed: uninterested women tolerate sex as a wifely duty and 'respectable' men regularly visit prostitutes and keep mistresses. Any suggestion of role reversal would have been scandalous. Granville Barker, like Shaw, believed in new morality but refused to perpetuate the tradition. Armed with self-knowledge, Ann defies social censure and rightly points out that her marriage with a gardener would not be opposed if they were alone in the world. As her sister's marriage of convenience ends up as a burnt-out case she refuses to accept it as unavoidable: '... if one can provide for oneself, or is independent, why get married!'[2] she retorts. His women break away from the pattern of female sexuality as interpreted by the patriarchy. Male sexuality also gets a different treatment: men in his plays are not heroic in proportion to their sexual drive; on the contrary, good and positive characters like Philip and Edward are least biologically driven; the bad ones like Lord John Carp and Trebell come to grief because of their unrestrained sexual urge. They are the 'spiritual sloven' who enjoy being unhappy. Barker also avoided extremes in his characterisation; none of his women are either excessively 'virtuous' or 'fallen'—a judicious balance between the two makes them more credible. With the emergence of Shaw and Granville Barker on the dramatic scene, much of the traditional male notion of female sexuality was subjected to challenge and transformation.

Like Shaw, Granville Barker also realised that the sexual role was one of the causes of women's bondage, but he did not overtly champion androgyny as Shaw and later Virginia Woolf did. His best men and women show a healthy coalescence of male and female elements in their personalities. This distrust of sexuality is expressed by Philip Madras in *The Madras House* (1911): 'I do so hate that farmyard world of sex—men and women always treating each other in this unfriendly way.'[3] Jessica, his fiancée, also regards it as an impediment to a harmonious relationship, but with reluctance accepts it because she loves him. When Philip talks about sexual differences she comments: 'You do make me forget I am a female, occasionally.'[4] Margery Morgan noted this 'androgynous temperament' and traced it to the influence of his dominating mother.[5] Holroyd held a similar view of Shaw. But, both these critics fail to perceive the consistency of the New Woman's philosophy: to secure the central role on the stage, represent the new morality and join the spiritual reform of society. The assertive women of Greek drama or even Shakespeare did not have this mission to transform the 'ugly, stupid, wasteful world' into a better one. This new moral passion urges Jessica in *The Madras House* to identify with a common woman whose body is being sold on the street or one who shot another poor devil. It is acknowledged that a price has to be paid for 'free womanhood.' In *The Wicked Man*, Elizabeth is proud of her womanhood but comments that it still has to depend on the use men put to it. The women, therefore, develop their endearing feminine traits. Ann calls it 'a joy of service.'

Granville Barker strikes the keynote of the new drama in the very opening scene of *The Madras House*: '... the two most important things ... attitude towards money and ... women.' In the first major work of criticism which attempted to do justice to the dramatist, *A Drama of Political Man: A Study in the Plays of Granville Barker*, Margery Morgan discovered the political consciousness of this talented dramatist who is chiefly concerned with society as it spans and transcends time and becomes civilisation. She wrote: 'His heroes reach, or fail to reach, the fulfilment of their moral being in the public realm; if they seem to move within a domestic circle, still their decisions are made in awareness of their political significance.'[6] She took note of 'the political virtue of honour' of Barker's heroes and their self-realization in public career, but she failed to appreciate the essential moral nature of his characters; nor did she notice his preoccupation with the status of women. C.B. Purdom's standard biography treated Barker's life as the tragedy of a man who lacked self-knowledge and wasted his energy in pursuit of illusory goals. Such a biased view has been recently corrected by Eric Salmon's *Granville Barker: A Secret Life* which helps us to understand his motives. His retirement from active stage work was a natural move to find more time for writing, and he had realised by that time that doing both was not possible. Moreover, his dream of a national theatre which he had cherished for over fifteen years was shattered by World War I. His timely marriage to Helen Hunnington in 1918 also helped him financially to settle down to writing. In 1907 he had published *A National Theatre: Scheme and Estimates*, an economical work of impressive detail but the project never became a reality. His own struggle is reflected in the struggle of his heroines against the oppressions of patriarchy, often without much success, but they put up an impressive resistance.

The apparent theme of Barker's first solo play *The Marrying of Ann Leete* is the sexual harassment of a woman by a man of superior position, but it owes much of its success to the challenge offered by his heroine to the false values of a decadent society. In her recent introduction to the Methuen Drama Series of *Granville Barker's Plays: One* (1993) Margery Morgan rather belatedly notes this characteristic: 'All the plays Barker had written before *The Voysey Inheritence* have a woman as a central character, who grows towards an understanding of herself and the world, and an acceptance of responsibility.'[7] The assertive heorines of Barker owe their existence to the New Women of the stage with whom he had interaction as a director and an actor. He successfully directed Lillah McCarthy for *Man and Superman* and many other plays and finally married her in 1906 to carry on their active partnership in the theatre. Like Philip, the hero of *The Madras House*, Barker possessed a 'reformer's mind' and intensely desired to ameliorate the moral fabric of Edwardian society. Being Everyman's art, drama could, he believed, have greater impact on people than other forms of art. The Vedrenne-Barker management of the Court Theatre (October 18, 1904-January 29, 1907) attempted to substitute the romantic comedy and melodrama with serious drama in pursuit of truth and a healthy intellectual entertainment.

Barker saw sexual passion as a destructive force as is evident from *Waste*. He segregated it from love and regarded it as an unreliable bond between man and woman. Ann Leete begins her marital life with a request to her husband to treat her as mother of his children rather than as a wife. The hero of *The Madras House* is vocal in his denunciation of the 'farm-yard world of sex.' Granville Barker's personal experience harmonized with the Freudian theory of sublimation of sex for artistic purpose. His close friend C.E. Wheeler accused him of denying any value to love as he confused physical appetite with love. This led to an oversimplification of sexuality in marriage as a degrading factor, and comradeship in work as the true ideal. His marriage with Lillah survived only for ten years in spite of closely working together and sharing the same interests. He asked for divorce as marital discord became counterproductive. Lillah resisted fiercely as her pride was badly hurt, but after a lot of persuasion the divorce was granted in 1918. Though Barker was attracted to the outspoken and vivacious personality of Lillah, he found enduring love and rapport in the reserved and quiet Helen.

Farewell to the Theatre, a one-act play, reveals a turning point in his career and personal life. On the one hand it expressed his desire to retire from the world of the performing arts to enter the world of scholarship, on the other it was a testament to the petering out of his conjugal love with his first wife and the beginning of a tender relationship with Helen culminating in marriage. The turmoil of his soul was reflected in the outright rejection by Dorothy, the aging actress, of the comforts of the fireside and financial security of the well-mannered world and the unfulfilled ambition of living upto the vision of 'better things than we are'. She rejects her former lover's proposal because of her awareness of her limitations. She is full of self-reproach because of her 'silly, self-conscious selves ... poor prisoners ... born to an evil time.' This uneasy conscience invests Granville Barker's heroines with a spiritual quality.

Barker's life was dominated by elderly women possibly because of the strong influence of his mother. He fell in love with Helen Hunnington, wife of a multimillionaire who was ten years older than him. During the twenty years of her uneventful marriage with Archer Hunnington she made a name as a minor novelist and poet. In April 1918 she accompanied Barker to England after arranging legal precedures for divorce. Barker made another renewed effort to achieve a meaningful relationship based on 'working together' and transcend physical desire. It was fortunate for him that Helen's divorce was generously settled. The financial stability helped the couple to embark on a life of scholarship and get married on July, 31, 1918.

Eric Salmon disagreed with Margery Morgan's thesis that Barker's plays are essentially political. He argued that the accent in his plays '... seems the exact reverse of Miss Morgan's statement. To find their reality, his characters move neither in a public-political nor in a private domestic sphere but in a secret world of their own ...'.[8] The protagonists, especially women, derive their strength from within which is extra-ordinary if we take into consideration the conservative atmosphere of the Edwardian era. So both the interpretations suffer from a partial view. With a rare determination and resilience, the heroines fight the various social corruptions which refutes the Freudian concept of the weak Superego in women and the inferior morality of their sex. Like H.G. Wells, Barker believed that the so-called advanced society reached a point of stagnation and exhaustion; it desperately needed to be injected with new bold ideas for its survival. And this typical *fin-de-siècle* spirit finds expression in his plays. Barker was bold enough to explore the various ramifications of sexual relationship on the outcome of the plays and its impact on the public as well as the personal life of the characters. However, his plays are political in the sense that the transformation of society including the improvement of women's status was aimed at. The spirituality of Barker's women has little association with any belief in God or the church; they fight alone, often a losing battle, against the hitherto unchallenged male supremacy and the decaying culture of Edwardian society. His interest in the Woman Question, however, did not lead to any scandalous affair. On the contrary, his lack of personal involvement with the opposite sex led his close associates like Norman Marshall and C.E. Wheeler to conjecture about his homosexual leanings. Both Barker and Shaw seem to have been influenced by the sublimation theory of transformation of sexual energy into higher channels of creativity advocated by Nietzsche, Novalis and Schopenhauer which later became a part of Freudian theory. Barker's anti-heroes are often caught up in a vortex of untamed libido mixed up with the ambition to move up the social ladder. They follow the dictates of their lust and are destroyed in the process. But the women seem to transcend the basic instincts and transmute them into a spiritual strength.

In *The Marrying of Ann Leete* the political opportunism of the father is atoned for by the moral integrity of the daughter. With all his diplomacy and cunning Carnaby Leete seeks power but fails to achieve his political ambition; Ann's straightforward dealings coupled with self-knowledge lead to a life of fulfilment and happiness. In the play George calls Ann a 'new woman' for her individuality, and the courage to make decisions about her own life and willingness to accept the consequences. The twenty-year-old girl is pitted against the cynicism and disintegrity of Lord John Carp and Carnaby Leete. The father, a fence-sitter willing to join the bandwagon of the Tories, uses his daughter to arrest his sinking political fortune. The experienced man of power-politics kisses Ann to win a bet and later offers to marry her to obviate any scandal which might jeopardize his political career. The proposal of the thoughtless politician is curtly turned down by the honest and sensitive girl—a humbling experience for the senior man that serious matters like marriage need at least a year to think over. Barker handles the young virgin as skilfully as he delves into the psyche of the politicians with their mid-life crises. Ann shows her emotional maturity by not fussing over the kiss but telling the impulsive lover that she bears no love for him and his proposal is ridiculous.

Barker explores the problem of sexuality in *The Marrying of Ann Leete* by focusing on the mental growth of the female protagonist who transcends her initial sexual embarrassment to become an independent and mature person who can follow her conscience in defiance of social pressures. Barker avoids the big events of romantic well-made plays to concentrate on the inner experience of a woman—an inheritance of 'the difference of view and the difference of standard', in Virginia Woolf's words. It is this feminine perspective that precludes Barker's women from being just clones of Shavian women. Being less articulate, they assert themselves more through action than speech. Both Major Barbara and Ann find themselves in ideological opposition to their corrupt but influential fathers: the eloquent Barbara after a stiff resistance finally joins her father to carry on her reform work but the quiet Ann proves herself a reservoir of strength when she resists the insinuations of her father and embarks on an experimental marriage with the family gardener. The shift in emphasis from the socially important protagonist to the ordinary person of merit is noteworthy. Ann's admission of being kissed by Lord John shows her conquest of the fear of scandal. Throughout the play she maintains a no-nonsense approach to love and sex. Like Webster's Duchess of Malfi she marries a person beneath her social status and willingly suffers the censure and ostracization. The New Women in Ibsen's plays often achieve freedom with irresponsibility; Shaw at times so mixed up his serious message with charlatanism and an overdose of wit, but Barker's women improve their status through persistent struggle and a dignified self-recognition.

Ann's frankness causes her embarrassment, but her sincerity and straight forwardness sharply contrasts with Lord John's philandering nature and insensitive attitude. Her solemn manner has an overpowering effect on the adventurous politician. Her sound commonsense helps her to see through her father's game and she is capable of making her own assessment of her future with a politician of shady character. But Ann's decision is more intuitive than intellectual; she turns the search within and is gifted with an insight into the motivation of the characters. This intelligent woman progressively discovers that their mutual attraction is not sufficiently strong to endure the strains of a lifelong marriage. Her further discovery of resemblance between John and her father only strengthens her ambivalence towards him. She is caught up in a dilemma between her duty to her father who was passing through a trying time and her own self. She emerges with a clear conscience unlike her sister Sarah who was also married off for the political convenience of her father. Though sexually exploited, she refuses to be another step on the ladder for her ambitious father. Unlike the conventional women of her time she belongs to the mental plane as is evident from her speech to George, 'I want to take people mentally.'[9]

Ann not only takes people as a challenge but also life itself. Her choice of the family gardener as her marriage partner involves a risk and a sacrifice of creature comforts. But she is mentally prepared for this experiment and resolves to bear with any unfortunate fall-out. Sarah's unhappy marriage has taught her to take charge of her own life and not to allow class distinctions to obfuscate her judgement. With Abud—an amiable man with spontaneous joy in man and nature—she feels more secure than with the veteran politician with all the trappings of power. She is confident that her decision would not seem irrational if her marriage survived. Barker added the Fourth Act to show the aftermath of her decision—a fairly happy marriage based on equality and mutual respect. Ann expresses her rebellion against the decaying influence of Edwardian commercialism and the disguised Philistinism of the upper class: '... we've all been in too great a hurry getting civilized. False dawn, I mean to go back.'[10] It is the courage to live her life according to her convictions that raises her to the status of the protagonist. The heroes no longer have the heroic roles; Abud has a submissive and minor role to play; John Carp emerges as a symbol of decadence.

In England feminism was first applied to campaigning for women's votes in 1890s. It was only in the late 1960s that feminine uniqueness was stressed rather than mere equality with men. Granville Barker's heroines possess this special quality of feminine uniqueness. New heroines like Ann and Jessica strengthen women's position rather than compete with men. The French socialist Charles Fourier who invented the word 'feminism' believed that the new woman would create a society based on association and mutuality rather than competition and profits. Almost half a century before the women's liberation movement, Granville Barker created stage roles for New Women who value self-unfoldment as the highest goal; they defy social conventions and risk being branded as unrespectable for the sake of their inner convictions. In *The Marrying of Ann Leete* Barker offers a faithful picture of women's oppression in England where daughters are married off to secure the political advantage of the father; respectable men bet on a young woman's ability to walk in a garden passage without screaming; the middle-aged Lord John thinks kissing a young lady against her will is worth bragging about. The naturalism of Barker did not permit creation of characters like Shaw's Candida and Ann who could push men about at will. His women struggle within the prison of Victorian-Edwardian society.

From the hypocrisy of a political turncoat Barker turned his attention to the unscrupulousness—a financial scam—of a solicitor's firm which has been exploiting its gullible clients for generations. He explores the dichotomy between the private conscience and public morality and interweaves the Woman's Question with the fortunes of a family. Edward learns from his father that the affluence of their family came from the fraudulent practice of using the client's fund for private gain. The crisis is reached when he resolves to disinherit the troubled legacy and face the legal consequence of his confession to the clients who reposed their trust in the Voyseys. In *The Voysey Inheritance* the role of the heroine is a supportive one. In the final Act of the play she helps the hero make the most momentous decision of his life: to confess the truth and face prosecution rather than be blackmailed by a few corrupt investors.

The play begins as a typical Edwardian Morality about tainted money and explores the theme of the sins committed by fathers being visited on their children. From the moral obsession it evolves into an existential philosophy of acceptance of responsibility and co-operation between man and woman in work and decision-making. From the very outset Alice proves herself a woman of substance by her ironical protest: 'Oh, I am lawless by birth-right, being a woman.'[11] The New Woman not only leads Edward to the path of expiation but also stands by him in his crucial hour and offers to marry him when his life is threatened by prosecution for swindling. A balanced and pragmatic woman, Alice persuades Edward to convene a meeting of all clients and confess the crime perpetrated for generations.

Arabella Kenealy argued in *Feminism and Sex-Extinction* that the feminist endangered reproduction of healthy children by denying women's uniqueness and too much insistence on equality with men. In *The Marrying of Ann Leete* femininity is extolled and Ann rejects the male symbolic order in the name of sexual difference. In *The Voysey Inheritance* we have a deconstructive approach: Alice attains equal status in the sphere of serious professional decision-making, hitherto usually a prerogative of the male. She sets aside the age-old dichotomy between the male and the female role and manages the family crisis with considerable dexterity. As the masterful and domineering Mr. Voysey could not undo the financial scam of his father, innocent Edward has to bear the brunt. Though Edward is the hero of the play, a brief but dominant role is played by Alice, the hero's fiancee. By virtue of her superior intelligence and natural leadership she seizes a significant position in the play. Without arrogance and fuss about 'the duel of sex' she becomes an influencing factor and a complementary force when the hero breaks down under the pressure of cricumstances. The negative outlook of the depressed hero is counterbalanced by her positive outlook. Throughout the play she maintains her autonomous status: she turns down the proposal of a 'well-principled prig' but offers her hand when he assumes his natural self. The source of her inner strength and confidence is her self-knowledge: 'I prefer my plan. I always do what I know I want to do.[12] Marriage is not the only goal for this New Woman; nevertheless she prefers the womanly 'joy of service.' With a level-headed pragmatism she finds a way out of the problem of preserving integrity in the face of financial corruption which eludes the high-principled Edward. As the sole executor of the firm when Edward suggests privation of the family and martyrdom for himself to compensate for the stolen money, Alice corrects his propriety by her good-humoured satire: 'Please don't glory in your martyrdom.[13] She shows remarkable emotional maturity under the stress and tension of everyday life. With a rare insight she perceives that Edward's obsession with morality was doing him more harm than good. Shaw's *Widowers' Houses* has a more or less similar situation. Blanche cures the hero's puritanical contempt for tainted money by her wit, sexual charm and occasional outbursts. But Barker's heroines like Alice and Jessica do not overpower their heroes either by their intellect or by their negative emotions. Alice suggests restoring the small investors' fund with available money at the cost of big clients. Unsure and indecisive, Edward acts upon her advice without being imposed upon. His lingering hesitation is finally blown away by the new moral codes of this New Woman. She persuades him to become a bad man and assert his natural aggressive self.[14] She goes about quietly to reform this 'spiritual sloven' by changing his perception. The cursed burden of disgrace has awakened his assertive nature and aroused an interest in poor humanity which he as been neglecting so far.

The hapless hero is rejuvenated by Alice's philosophy of faith: 'Edward, I have a faith by which I hope to live, not humbly but by defying the world to be my master. Dare to surrender yourself entirely, and you'll find them powerless against you.'[15] This mature vision of life leads to a reciprocal love and understanding which transcends the moral issues of the day. Alice surpasses Beatrice, a clever woman as hard as nails who is trapped in a marriage of convenience. In *The Voysey Inheritance* Barker successfully elevates women's position from the stereotyped sex-role to an autonomous and responsible role at par with the male characters. The New Women of Bernard Shaw stole the limelight because of their intelligent, unemotional, physically robust nature and the ingenious role reversal by the dramatist. But the heroines of Granville Barker do not conform to the masculine stereotypes: in moments of crises they act from a position of strength and quietly assert themselves. Their androgynous behaviour is quite consistent with modern psychological theory that adults need the positive characteristics of both the masculine and feminine stereotypes to function smoothly in society. Barker's achievement lies in balancing the overdose of passivity and emotional dependence of the Victorian women.

In *Waste* Granville Barker turns his attention from financial bankruptcy to moral bankruptcy. He shows the oppression of women as well as their struggle to liberate themselves. Trebell, the promising politician gets entangled in an extramarital affair with the charming wife of Justin O'Connell. His well-intentioned Disestablishment Bill to dissociate the power of the church from corrupting the world of politics is ruined by his lack of self-knowledge and misunderstanding of female sexuality. What is casual philandering for Trebell is serious involvement for Amy. The rest of the plot is a vortex of misplaced emotion and relentless pursuit of political ambition. Unrestrained passion leads an otherwise sincere politician to a debacle in his career and a tragedy in his personal life. Emotionally starved Amy turns to Trebell for the loving tenderness she misses in her incompatible marriage. To Trebell the affair is no more than the gratification of a passing sexual passion; for Amy it is a heartrending struggle for the possession of a powerful man's heart. Her growing awareness of this attitudinal difference makes her wonder 'Why can't women take love affairs so lightly?'[16] The busy politician who looks upon love and courtship as a waste of time is unaware of the spiritual need that compels Amy to pursue happiness at the risk of scandal. She aims at controlling her lover: 'It would do you good to fall really desperately in love with me ... to give me the power to make you happy.'[17] But Trebell proves to be too self-centred to provide the mental and emotional security she needs; Amy discovers his unloving nature only after becoming pregnant. Political expediency and fear of a possible political scandal prompts him to a cover-up operation. Amy, on the other hand, sticks to her feminine point of view: 'I want affection now just as I want food. I can't do without it.... I can't reason things out as you can.'[18]

This enunciation of women's predicament from a woman's perspective makes Barker a dramatist of rare class. The tough world of politics is in conflict with the sensitivity of an imaginative woman. The difference in outlook is again highlighted when she regards their union as a unique moment of lifetime whereas Trebell looks back on that night as on 'a fit of drunkness.' The antagonism gradually heightens till it drives Amy to total desperation. With the realisation that their relationship would never culminate in marriage, she declares an open rebellion on the Machiavellian hero and rejects his entreaty to give birth to his illegitimate child. Though reduced to the position of a victim, she asserts her right to choose. In this secret warfare between unequal powers she proves her mettle by challenging Trebell's insinuation and winning the polemical battle over the right to self-determination: 'Your choices in life have made you what you want to be, haven't they? Leave me mine.'[19] The abstract and evasive metaphysics of the wily politician seems too tenuous to withstand her clear reasoning. Her refusal to bear Trebell's child is neither vindictive nor impulsive: a premonition about her child's insecure future leads her to abortion. Her agonised cry of protest is the cry of every Victorian—Edwardian woman: 'You drive us to distraction and sometimes to death by your stupidities. Poor women!'[20] Her prolonged depression and final suicide spells the doom of the politician. The woman he underestimates as 'nothingness ... silly ... vain' proves a fatal force after her death. The political career for which he sacrificed two lives is ruined; the Disestablishment Bill remains a dream. The political maturity of the hero is offset by his conventional morality. Had he listened to the voice of reason—the new morality of this New Woman—the precious lives as well as the beneficial Bill might have survived. While the New Woman in *The Marrying of Ann Leete* and *The Voysey Inheritance* has positive roles to play, in *Waste* her destructive power is displayed. Julia's comment on the suicide of the hero under the burden of guilt and remorse is illuminating. If men knew one woman from another, she remarked, the tragic waste could have been avoided.

In his theoretical work *On Dramatic Method* Barker argued: 'One of the signs of the true dramatist is that his characters, at first, seem to leap from the pages at you.'[21] Undoubtedly his women characters fit this description. The plot and incidents may fade from memory but the personalities of Ann and Amy live on. After dealing with the destructive power of sex Granville Barker explores its sublimation. The opening scene of *The Madras House* overtly raises the Woman Question: 'Well my dear Tommy, What are the two most important things in a man's character? His attitude towards money and his attitude towards women.'[22] This concern for women's position is further sustained by Mr. State who wants to buy up the drapery business in order to make a significant contribution to women's causes. Moreover, the hero's father Constantine Madras was converted to Mohamedanism because he thought it offered greater dignity and privileges to women. Major women characters show considerable growth compared to the static male characters. Even a minor character like Miss Yates, a shop assistant with little education shows exceptional degree of courage and independence of mind. She foils all attempt to elicit the name of her child's father on the ground that it was her personal business. The irrepressible spinster decides to leave her job and raise the child unaided which makes Barker comment in the stage direction: 'She has genius—she has life,... And commoner people are lustreless beside her.'[23] Granville Barker finds the model New Woman in Jessica whom he describes thus: '... Philip's wife is an epitome of all that aesthetic culture can do for a woman: More: she is the result—not of thirty-three years—but of three or four generations of cumulative refinement.'[24] Despite such refinement and culture she is not reduced to the position of a romantic heroine-on-the-pedestal or the doll-wife. With a charming, delicate, sensitive wife by his side Philip explores a spiritual companionship as a substitute for sexual gratification. Together they come to 'hate that farm-yard world of sex—men and women always treating each other in this unfriendly way.'[25]

Shaw delights in the battle of the sexes but Barker treats it as something unnatural and aims at its sublimation: 'We have so organised the world's work as to make companionship between men and women a very artificial thing.'[26] As a positive move towards his goal, he decides to stand for the county council. Jessica not only appreciates the spirit of sacrifice but also actively co-operates with him to cut down on the luxuries and achieve happiness through austerities. She leads him on the right track sometimes by criticizing his attempt to 'seduce everybody to [his] own way of thinking'. Together they are inspired and committed to ameliorate he '... ugly, stupid wasteful world'. As Philip's great revolution begins at home, he cannot succeed without Jessica's help. As a team they endeavour to usher in 'an ... art and a culture that shan't be just a veneer on savagery ... but it must spring in good time from the happiness of a whole people.'[27] In *The Madras House* Barker achieves a fine balance between art and social responsibility. And women play a new active role in it. From the stereotyped image of victims women begin to emerge as a decisive force. In their high sense of moral responsibility they are closer to the existentialists. As to Jessica, Barker highlights her 'lady-like arrogance' and her acceptance of the challenge 'to face the new future.' Margery Morgan's assessment of her character in the introduction as 'the most negative and cold-hearted character in the whole play'[28] is unjustly and unnecessarily biased. She is equal to Alice in understanding and co-operation with which she rescues the hero from deep crisis. The subtlety of Granville Barker's plays was appreciated by J.B. Priestley, the eminent playwright and critic, in the Foreward to his collected plays: '... he is undoubtedly one of the most original, intelligent and sensitive dramatists of the century, who often takes Shavian themes but scores them for an orchestra and not for Shaw's military band.'[29]

Feminism as a political movement began in the late 1960s, but in dramatic literature the New Woman emerged much earlier in the plays of Shaw in 1890s and further developed in the hands of Granville Barker during early twentieth century. Under Ibsen's influence these playwrights of the dramatic revival inducted New Women as heroines who dare to reject the male symbolic order and carve their own niche against all odds. They raise the traditional status of women from nonentities to active decision-makers. Heroines like Alice and Jessica are more sensible and sensitive than romantic. They come down from the pedestal and work with the heroes as equal partners. Tragic women like Amy show by their suffering the futility of patriarchal domination. Charles Fourier and Karl Marx maintained that the extent of social progress is best measured by the extent of women's freedom. In the words of Simone de Beauvoir: 'One is not born, but rather becomes a woman, no biological, psychological or economic fate determines the figure that the human female presents.'[30] The heroines of Barker's plays wage a battle against this conditioning. Feminists have criticised psycho-analytic theories for using male sexuality as the norm and then measuring the differences of female sexuality against it; they refer to it as 'phallocentrism': Female sexuality has either been theorized as a riddle or a problem or is seen merely in terms of the process of procreation. Barker's plays are surprisingly free from this bias. His women are not judged by a male standard: they are courageous in their own way. Even as a victim of an 'adulterous and sterile generation' Amy fares better than the tragic heroine of John Masefield's *The Tragedy of Nan* who kills her lover to prevent him from stealing the compensation money provided by the court. The double standard and corruption of Edwardian society is somewhat mitigated by the compensating integrity of the women. Amelia, the deserted wife of Constantine Madras in *The Madras House* remains faithful to the husband who embraced Mohamedanism for the privilege of polygamy. Like some Shakespearean heroines, Alice, Jessica and Ann are more emotionally mature than the heroes—hence they guide and control them. They also influence the action of the plays. The New Women in Shaw's plays fight the injustice at the intellectual level; the heroines of Granville Barker are average, down-to-earth women with extraordinary moral and spiritual strength. Their serious nature is a manifestation of the playwright's serious concern for the struggle that was going on to transform women's lives. The talented actresses, weary of the puerile theatre of the day, responded competently to the challenging roles. Women are instrumental in debunking politics and politicians—the agents of corruption. Ironically, their search for personal power and profit is ruthlessly exposed by women, apparently insignificant pawns in their power game. All the women show greater understanding of human life and the psychology of the opposite sex. Consciously or otherwise Granville Barker created this new force to represent his view of the Woman Question. The aging actress, Dorothy, in *Farewell to Theatre* evinces great dissatisfaction with 'the catlike comfort of the fireside, the shelter of cheque book' and rejects the limitations of 'the silly, self-conscious selves'[31] to work for a better world. It is a pity that the women characters of Shaw have been subjected to the extremes of adulation and disparagement, those of Granville Barker have sunk into oblivion.

NOTES AND REFERENCES

1. Dennis Kennedy, ed., *Plays by Granville Barker* (London, Cambridge Un. Press, 1993), p. 57.
2. *Ibid.*, p. 106.
3. *The Madras House* (London, Methuen, 1977), p. 136.
4. *Ibid.*, p. 137.

5. *Ibid.*, p. 5.
6. Margery Morgan, *Granville Barker: A Drama of Political Man* (London, Sidwick & Jackson, 1961), p. 6.
7. *Granville Barker; Plays; One*, (London, Methuen, 1993), p. xxvii.
8. Eric Salmon, *Granville Barker: A Secret Life*, (London, Heinemann. 1983), p. 36.
9. *Plays by Granville Barker* (London, Cambridge Un., 1993), p. 56.
10. *Ibid.*, p. 82.
11. *Ibid.*, p. 128.
12. *Ibid.*, p. 105.
13. *Ibid.*, p. 127.
14. *Ibid.*, p. 157.
15. *Ibid.*, p. 158.
16. *Ibid.*, p. 176.
17. *Ibid.*, p. 175.
18. *Ibid.*, p. 189
19. *Ibid.*, p. 191.
20. *Ibid.*, p. 192.
21. Granville Barker, *On Dramatic Method* (N. York, Hill & Wang, 1956), p. 34.
22. *The Madras House* (London, Eyre Methuen, 1977), p. 5.
23. *Ibid.*, p. 38.
24. *The Madras House* (1911), p. 57.
25. *Ibid.*, p. 136.
26. *Ibid.*, p. 63.
27. *Ibid.*, p. 136.
28. *Ibid.*, p. xxviii.
29. *The Collected Plays of Harley Granville Barker*, Vol-I (London, Diswick & Jackson, 1967), p. 9.
30. Judith Okley, Trsl., *The Second Sex* (London, Virago, 1968), p. 90.
31. Quoted by Eric Salmon in *Granville Barker: A Secret Life* (London, Heinemann, 1983), p. 257.

JOHN GALSWORTHY: THE CONSCIENTIOUS WOMEN

5

Like Shaw and Barker, Galsworthy wrote serious plays to make the public think about social issues. A man of conservative outlook and artistic temperament, he avoided the blatant method of a preacher. The crowning glory of his career was the Nobel Prize, awarded for his fiction. As a plawright he is remembered for his 'warm humanity' and sympathetic identification with his weak and oppressed characters. Though not known to be a feminist, he shows a deep concern about women's position and problems. He advocated votes for women and campaigned for the revision of Divorce Laws so as to facilitate dissolution of unhappy marriages without the pretence of adultery. He even supported the cause of London prostitutes who moved him to pity.

While writing plays he could not remain unaffected by the spirit of the new drama. Well-known playwrights like Pinero and Jones had raised questions about the subjugation and exploitation of women but they always ended their plays with a reinforcement of patriarchal values to appease the Victorian audience. The breakthrough was achieved by Shaw, Archer and Granville Barker who championed Ibsen's ideas with their translations and performances. Despite his denials of any influence writings of Ibsen or Shaw, Galsworthy refined the art of naturalism of the former and shared the moral earnestness of the latter. He dedicated his first plays *The Silver Box*, *Joy*, and *Strife* to Granville Barker who staged them successfully at the Court Theatre. His reputation was subject to fluctuation—from the trying years of the thirties to the oblivion of the forties. Some of the topical problems of his days may have become obsolete after a century, but the humanitarian approach to social problems is never likely to grow stale. Hence the fifties and sixties saw a revival of interest in his works which climaxed in 1967, the year of his birth centenary. He was hailed as a reformer and a humanist but his contribution to women's causes still remains unappreciated. His New Woman and a new interpretation of sexual morality deserve close study.

After his initial start with woman as a hunted species in *The Silver Box*, Galsworthy attempted to created a New Woman in *Joy*—a deserted wife with a problem adolescent daughter who develops a strong aversion for her mother's lover. In this psychological battle of nerves, she wins her autonomy and breaks away from the image of the submissive woman. The play was not well received by the public possibly because of the uncoventional characterization and the triumph of the assertive woman who rejects the Victorian virtue of self-denial. He had to wait for another five years before he could create another unconventional woman of courage and convictions in *The Eldest Son*.

Galsworthy's women characters have received less than their share of critical attention. Even after his so-called rehabilitation, little beyond his early problem plays like *The Silver Box*, *Strife* or *Justice* is known to the public. There has not been much serious study of his middle and late plays. The image of a humanitarian artist and a problem playwright has eclipsed much of his novelty in characterization and experiments in somewhat subversive plays such as *Joy*, *The Eldest Son*, *The Fugitive*, *The Skin Game*, and *Windows*. Alardyce Nicoll admitted that Galsworthy's art of arousing sympathy was dramatically more effective than Shaw's scintillating wit and laughter.[1] Their approach to social problems is different. To Shaw, prostitution, for example, was a manifestation of economic exploitation of women. Galsworthy simply treated it as an evidence of the immorality of men as expressed in *Escape*: 'Clean streets'—that's the cry. Clean men! That would be better.'[2] This humanitarian attitude and insistence on justice for the weak and the oppressed would have made him a Human Rights activist in the present age.

The new drama of Shaw, Granville Barker and Galsworthy inducted the angry young woman in the same way as the new drama of Pinter and Osborne introduced the 'angry young man' in the 1950s. The advancement in women's position is obvious from a comparative study of Pinero's tame ending in *The Case of Rebellious Susan* in which women conclude: '...we poor women cannot retaliate'[3] and Galsworthy's emancipated wives like Mrs. Gwyn, Mrs. Builders and Mrs. Strangway who desert their husbands without any qualms or indeed, without tragic consequences. 'Rebellious' Susan who sets out to pay back her philandaring husband in his own coin is finally manipulated to fit into the stereotyped Victorian wife. In 'The New Woman and the Problem Plays' Catherine Wiley criticized Pinero and Jones for their conservative portrayal of the New Woman. She took them to task for focusing on what the heroine does rather what she is.[4] The assertive wives of Galsworthy's plays demonstrate that desertion need not be a male monopoly.

Edwardian drama cannot be discussed without reference to its moral outlook. In *Some Platitudes Concerning Drama* (1909) Galsworthy says: 'Now, in writing plays, there are, in this matter of moral, three courses open to the serious dramatist. The first is: To definitely set before the public that which it wishes to have set before it, the views and codes of life by which the public lives and in which it believes.[5] The plays of Pinero and Jones with their conventional ending belong to this category. 'The second course is: To definitely set before the public those views and codes of life which the dramatist himself believes, the more effectively if they are opposite of what the public wishes to have placed before it, presenting them so that the audience may swallow them like powder in a spoonful of jam.'[6] The plays of Bernard Shaw fit this description. Galsworthy then proceeds to define a third category: 'There is a third course: To set before the public no cut-and-dried codes, but the phenomena of life and character, selected and combined, *but not distorted*, by the dramatist's outlook, set down without fear, favor, or prejudice, leaving the public to draw such poor moral as nature may afford.'[7] Ibsen and Galsworthy shared this approach. The latter criticized the stale morality of the commercial drama: 'The moral of the average play is now, and probably has always been, the triumph at all costs of a supposed immediate ethical good over a supposed immediate ethical evil.'[8]

Galsworthy's personal as well as literary life was dominated by a New Woman who not only inspired him to be a professional writer but also typed his manuscripts and offered valuable advice. Ada Galsworthy (née Cooper) found herself sexually incompatible with Arthur, and did not share his overriding passion for the army. She was introduced to John through his sisters, and found in him the tenderness and understanding she missed in her marriage. By 1895 they were lovers but John had to wait till she was granted divorce. Her marital crisis finds expression in the unhappily married women characters like Irene and Clare who evince violent repulsion to sexual relationship with their detested husbands. Galsworthy's love-affair with a married woman and his lasting marriage is similar to John Stuart Mill's liasion with Mrs. Harriet Taylor.

The other New Woman, who influenced him profoundly was Margaret Morris, a lively dancer of 19 whose youthful charm infatuated Galsworthy in his mid-forties. Margaret fell deeply in love with his magnetic personality and continued to love him till the end of her life. Galsworthy unconsciously wrote the part of Mrs. Megan for her in *The Pigeon*. Initially both John and Ada took interest in her career and often invited her. Margaret was a woman with a new morality and naively expected Ada to accept the fact that her role as a mistress posed no threat to her marriage. Although John and Ada believed in love without possessiveness, they could not live upto this high principle. For John it was a dilemma: inwardly he needed the stimulation and youthful exuberance of Margaret for his creativity, but he was too sensitive to betray his lifelong loyalty to Ada. The unresolved conflict resulted in a tense atmosphere which shadowed the final years of their conjugal life. The strain of their triangular affair has found a faithful expression in *The Dark Flower*. An extra-marital affair develops between the middle-aged hero and young Sylvia exactly like John's love for Margaret and ends with the hero's overnight decision to take the wife abroad to avoid the temptation of the young mistress. Margaret Morris wrote a candid account of her relationship with the playwright in *My Galsworthy Story*. She appeared to have thought it was a tragic error for Galsworthy to mar the threesome to appease Ada and smother his guilty conscience.

In his letter to Margaret dated 18th February 1912 Galsworthy expressed deep concern for Ada who still was his first priority: 'Her life and mine together has been such and our love has been and is such as to make it a sacred trust; and you are too dear and good not to feel with me that we cannot take happiness out of her despair and misery ... Forget, forget and forgive me.'[9] Margaret described Galsworthy as a lovable and kind person and loved his dynamic and passionate nature. She narrated how she was kissed by Galsworthy in a taxi and regretted that he went no further. She labelled her relationship with John and Ada the 'Eternal Triangle,'[10] and argued that much misery could be avoided if people realized that it is possible for one person to love two people at the same time. She wondered how any sensible person could be so conceited as to imagine that he or she could possibly satisfy the spiritual, mental, and physical needs of another individual completely. John's love transformed her whole life and she wanted to reciprocate by offering her youth and vitality to stimulate his creative power.

Apart from Ada and Margaret, other women who influenced him were his mother and sisters. His mother was a woman of exceptional courage and enterprise. She managed a big house with lots of servants and had little time to spend on her children. In awe the children turned to their father and avoided their stern mother. At the time of marriage his father was forty-five and mother twenty-five which explains their strained relationship. He had two sisters—Lilian and Mabel who kept close contact with their childless brother.

It is not unnatural therefore that the unhappy marriage and unconsummated love became a recurrent motif in his novels and plays. Irene Forsyte of *The Forsyte Saga*, for example, is based on Ada whom he met in Paris in 1895. Like Ada, Irene left her husband Soames Forsyte for a young man of congenial temparament. A parallel can be found between *The Fugitive* (1913) and his trilogy *The Forsyte Saga* (1922). The theme of a conscientious and rebellious heroine, fighting male hegemomy runs through these novels. Like Clare Dedmond, Irene battles to run away from her affluent husband Soames Foresyte, the unlovable and unheroic hero of the Saga. Though Soames is not a bad character, Irene would under no circumstances get reconciled to him. Readers may feel more pity for him and turn their animus to Irene for not forgiving him. But to her where sexual compatibility is lacking in one of the partners, 'no amount of pity, or reason or duty or what not, can overcome the repulsion implicit in Nature.'[11] *In Chancery* (1936) Soames' offer to Irene freedom, a separate house is bluntly refused: 'You may hunt me to the grave. I will not come.' is the flat answer. Irene's crusade begins with her refusal to be an object—the prized possession of charm and beauty for her husband and the Forsytes. Galsworthy writes in the Preface that the Saga is about 'a concretion of disturbing Beauty impinging on a possessive world[12] Irene is regarded as a misfit and a runaway wife who disgraced the Forsyte family.

The general belief in the family is that as a wife Irene brought nothing but trouble to everyone. Soames is made to suffer for years without even the benefit of divorce. His bovine attachment is matched only by her equally persistent apathy. Other male character like old Nicholas rapped out: 'Wives and daughters! There is no end to their liberty in these days.[13] A similar protest is heard from Timothy: 'The country's breaking up; I don't know what we're comin' to ... Too many women nowadays, and they don't know what they want.'[14] The suffocation caused by the Victorian prigs is to some extent relieved by old Joylon who describes himself as a feminist and does all within his power to promote Irene's happiness. He does not mince matters: 'I am against any woman living with any man whom she definitely dislikes. It appears to me rotten.'[15] He bequeaths a sum of £15000 free of legacy duty to Irene which gives her some financial independence.

Like the drama, the novels also deal with the problem of female sexuality. Like other typical virgins of his age Irene was also quite unprepared to cope with the realities of sex. Moreover, to an independent mind like Irene's, marriage did not necessarily equate with the right to sexual relationship. She could care for old Joylon; but could love only the artist Bosinney who died in a car accident. *The Man of Property* and other novels are a modern version of the Greek cycle of doom. According Ada Galsworthy, the figure of Irene is identified with the destructive power of Beauty.

To many the character of Irene is controversial. Though Galsworthy was writing about his own class, he neither glorified nor suppressed anything. In the Preface to *The Forsyte Saga* (1936) he sardonically predicted the doom of the middle class: 'If the upper-middle class, with other classes, is destined to 'move in' into amorphism, here pickled in these pages, it lies under glass for strollers in the wild and ill-arranged museum of Letters to gaze at. Here it rests, preserved in its own juice: The Sense of Property.'[16] D.H. Lawrence published an analysis of Galsworthy's novels in *Scrutinies*, 1928, which is not only acerbic but also a string of four-letter licentiousness. He first denied having met 'one single human individual.' All the Forsytes forfeit the right to be called 'human individuals'. 'They have lost that bit of free manhood and free womanhood which makes men and women.'[17] Every single character is determined by money; either the getting it, or having it, or the wanting it, or the utter lacking it. They are fallen, all social beings, a castrated lot. Even the love of Irene and Bosinney seems to him 'nothing but doggish amorousness and a sort of anti-Forsytism. ... Runaway dogs of these Forsytes, running in the back garden and furtively and ignominiously copulating—this is the effect on me, of Mr Galsworthy's grand love affairs.'[18]

Irene seems to him a 'sneaking, creeping, spiteful sort of bitch, an anti-Forsyte.... She is like a property mongrel doing dirt in the property kennels. But she is a real property prostitute, like the little model in *Fraternity*.'[19] He ridicules Galsworthy's handling of sex. It is when he comes to sex that Mr Galsworthy collapses finally. He becomes nastily sentimental. He wants to make sex important, and he only makes it repulsive. ... Very few people really feel love, or sex passion, or kindliness, or anything else that goes at all deep. So the mass just fake these feelings inside themselves. Fakes feelings! Woman is 'just a floating female sex organ, hovering round to satisfy his little hungers, and the *basta*. Anything of the real meaning of sex never occurs. It is a function, and the female is sort of sexual appliance, no more.'[20] Then came the volcanic lava of invectives: His treatment of passion is shameful. The whole thing is doggy to a degree. The temporary 'hunger' or the heat passes and so on. Lawrence laments, "Oh, if only Mr Galsworthy had satirized *this* side of Forsytism, the anti-Forsyte posturing of the 'rebel,' the narcissus and the exhibitionist, the dogs copulating on the pavement! Instead of that, he glorified it, to the eternal shame of English literature."[21]

Much of Lawrence's sarcasm is personal and judged in the light of his theory of sex. The steady readership and the Nobel award for the novels are proof enough of the merit of Galsworthy's characterization. Lawrence is incapable of appreciating the tenderness that is associated with the sexuality in Irene. The moral scruple of the characters is passed over to harangue on the crass commercialism of the day.

In his play, unhappily married women like Clare and Ruth Honeywill run away from their incompatible marriage but undergo undeserved hardship due to the rigidity of the Divorce Law and its male bias. Physical torture by a husband was not in itself sufficient ground for a wife to obtain divorce. His personal experience of a prolonged wait for nine years to marry Ada convinced him of women's suffering. Sympathetic characterization became the hall mark of Galsworthy's art. Like Ibsen and Shaw, he conceived the characters first and then developed the plot around them. He evolved the negative method of drawing characters from the average and below-average men and women who would reveal themselves, not from a heroic but a realistic point of view. The unheroic hero and vulnerable heroines of his early plays are well-known. But the wide range of Galsworthy's women characters has not been seriously considered by the critics. He depicts the evolution of women at different stages—at the bottom of the ladder are poor working-class wives like Mrs. Jones and Mrs. Roberts who have to pay a heavy price on account of some illegal and irrational action of their husbands—the typical fate of Victorian stereotypes. Two more victims of oppressive patriarchal society are Clare and Chloe who nevertheless put up a stubborn resistance. Haunted and hunted by class conflict Chloe commits suicide and Clare succumbs to death after having failed in her attempt to secure a suitable lover. Next in the hierarchy are working maids—Freda and Faith who are seduced by the young males of an upper-class family but rejected by their conservative fathers. The poor but resilient maids, for their part, turn down the offers of 'charity marriage' based on pity only.

In *Joy* the intelligent and assertive New Woman eschewed the traditional role which was nothing but a social construct. She brought with her a new morality. She was prepared to defy social codes and conventions wherever reason and good sense demanded this. She no longer allowed herself to be treated as the exclusive property of either father or husband. Mrs. Gwyn, Mrs. Builder and Mrs. Beatrice Strangway walked away from their unconsummated marriages without a guilty conscience. The plays are a quest for the economic independence and autonomy of women. Ibsen wrote in his 'Notes for the Modern Tragedy': 'There are two kinds of spiritual laws, two kinds of conscience, one in man and another, altogether different, in woman. They do not understand each other; but in practical life the woman is judged by man's law, as though she were not a woman but a man.'[22]

Galsworthy, the dramatist practised what Ibsen preached. Like his contemporaries he explored the problems of love and sexuality from an objective point of view. His subtle artistic method was closer to that of Granville Barker than that of Shaw who imposed his ideas on the audience with an old-fashioned violence. Moreover, he shared neither Shaw's economic outlook nor his belief in the theory of sublimation and the superman. In two early plays—*The Silver Box*, and *Strife* he showed the undeserved ordeal of two working-class wives. With *Justice* Galsworthy introduced the unhappy wife whose efforts to break away from a maladjusted marriage prove to be a move from the frying pan into the fire. Far from moralizing on women and their extra-martial affairs, he held up for scrutiny the rigidity and the double-standards of the Divorce Laws responsible for their tragedy. Pinero's *The Case of Rebellious Susan* ends with the author's opinion in the dedicatory epistle that as women cannot retaliate openly, they may retaliate secretly—and lie.'[23] The hypocrisy was so deep-seated in the Victorian mind that the manager of the Criterion, Charles Wyndham refused to allow the leading actress Mary Moor to utter the one line which would have confirmed Susan's adultery, in deference to the moral sentiment of the theatre—goers. But in real life he had an adulterous relationship with the same actress. Galsworthy did not subscribe to this kind of cant. The relative popularity of the playwrights, however, shows that late Victorian-Edwardian audience was still not ready for the 'new morality.' Figures of performances between 1890 and 1919 by the critic Ian Clarke indicate that Shaw's plays had 2568 performances while Jones notched up a total of 3690 and Pinero as much as 4834.[24] The plays of Galsworthy and Granville Barker were staged only 290 and 231 times. Shaw's plays overtook the commercial theatre only in the final years of the nineteenth century and reached wider audience beyond the intellectual elite.

In *Joy*, Galsworthy attempted a bold interpretation of love and sexuality. His new women belong to all classes. There are working girls without much education and refinement like Freda and Faith. He protrayed liberated middle-class wives like Mrs. Clare Dedmond, Mrs. Gwyn and Beatrice. Upper class New Women are Dot Chesire, Mrs. Builder and Mrs. March. Galsworthy's concern for social justice made him treat the extra-marital affairs of the unhappy wives as a natural outcome of incompatibility rather than occasions for a moral harangue.

The interrelationship between love and sexuality is a recurrent motif in Galsworthy's plays. But for him, love is more a matter of pity and sympathy than the irresistible attraction between the sexes. As a realist he did not depend on romance for theatrical success. Two of his early plays, *The Silver Box* and *Strife* were warmly received by the public and the critics. From his own experience of marriage with an unhappy wife, Galsworthy seems to have derived his compassionate view of love. The extra-marital love of his unhappy couples does not always end in tragedy as it always does in the plays of Pinero and Jones. Galsworthy's women do not set out to revolutionize the world like the intellectual women of Shaw. Theirs is a comparatively quiet battle. Love and sexuality are explored in *Joy* from the feminine point of view. Mrs. Gwyn, a deserted wife, not only asserts her right to have a lover, but cures her immature and obdurate teenage daughter's obsession with her mother. In a firm and dignified way the daughter is made to direct her attention to the fulfilment of her own love. Galsworthy turned to the theme of a woman's exigency of love in *Windows* which ends with a climactic epiphany for Mrs. March: Faith, her parlour maid with a criminal record of infanticide, would not compromise with anything short of love from her son. Galsworthy describes her transformation from a strict mother to a woman with compassion for another woman in distress: 'There is something unusual about her appearance, as if formality had dropped from her.' Her final speech is a revelation: 'I see it all. You-can't-help-unless-you-love.... She wants to be loved. It's the way of the world.'[25] In *The Eldest Son* a similar protest is registered by Freda, another lady's maid made pregnant by the eldest son of the Chesire family. She is determined to leave her job and suffer the consequences of her displacement rather than accept a loveless marriage. In spite of the encouragement of the feminist daughter of this aristocratic family, she would not consent to a marriage based on pity but devoid of love.

Women in Galsworthy's plays often appear unfortunate victims of circumstances or the hunted species. The suffering and social displacement of poor wives like Mrs. Jones,

Mrs. Roberts, Mrs. Ruth Honeywill and Mrs. Chloe is a faithful reflection of women's condition in Edwardian society. Galsworthy's implicit message is that their tragedy might have been averted if society had been a little merciful. Some women with greater will-power like Clare and Freda battle against an indifferent and relentless power, and often without much success. But their determined struggle against this oppressive force is an indication of the emergence of an unconventional type of female protagonist.

The third category consists of women like Dot, Mrs. Gwyn, Ann and Beatrice who openly revolt against the exploitation of their sex, and achieve moderate success. Dot, the feminist daughter of the conservative Cheshire family lashes out at the Victorian prudery in *The Eldest Son*: 'It's always like this, women kept in blinkers, roseleaves and humbug.'[26] She blames the snobbery of her family for Freda's predicament: 'Heaven help Freda, whatever she has done! I'd sooner be a private in a German regiment than a woman.'[27] She transcends class barriers and upholds the progressive view that a marriage should not bind a couple who no longer love each other.[28]

Galsworthy's treatment of love, marriage and sexuality is different from Shaw's. His New Women attempt a new and bold interpretation of sexuality. Shavian feminists like Lesbia and Lina scorn offers of marriage and are proud to be spinsters because marriage laws are absurd. But Galsworthy hints at the need for reform of Divorce Laws by depicting the undeserved suffering of the unhappy wives like Ruth Honeywill and Clare Dedmond who are deprived of the chance of a second marriage. The bias of the Divorce Laws in favour of men is obvious. Until 1857 divorce could be obtained through church courts and a special Act of Parliament was necessary before a divorce could be legalized. In consequence divorce was rare and could be afforded only by the rich and the influential. Adultery and cruelty were the accepted grounds; but the wife was commonly in an unfavourable position so that no divorce was granted on account of adultery till 1801. The law of 1857 added desertion as a ground—a fact duly taken note of by Mrs. Gwyn, in Galsworthy's *Joy*. It is only since 1938 that unsoundness of mind and the concept of 'marital break-down' were acceptable grounds. Emancipated wives like Clare Demond, Mrs. Builders and Beatrice Strangway show an awareness of 'marital breakdown' long before its enactment. The absence of a law forces them to the path of open revolt.

Moreover, Galsworthy never shared Shaw's theories of sublimation and Superman as the foundation of love and marriage. He treats sexuality as an essential part of the normal relationship between the sexes. His naturalism is closer to Ibsen's and Barker's than Shaw's. In *Some Platitudes Concerning Drama* he distinguished three types of dramatists. The first gives a view of life that the public desires; the second offers a view of life the dramatist believes; and the third presents a view, carefully selected but not distorted by the vision of the dramatist and leaves the public to draw its own conclusion.[29] Obviously, Shaw belongs to the second; Ibsen and Galsworthy to the third category.

An attitudinal shift in the status of women is important in these plays. A woman with a past is destroyed in *The Second Mrs. Tanqueray*; in *Windows*, a girl convicted for infanticide is condoned and rehabilitated by a respectable family. *A Family Man* shows the growing disillusionment of a domineering head of the family, John Builder who loses control over his wife and daughters. In a reversal of roles he is deserted not only by his wife and daughters but also by the French mistress whom he turns to in splendid isolation. The deserting wife and daughters neither return nor repent as in the typical ending of *The Case of Rebellious Susan* and *The Notorious Mrs. Ebbsmith*. These plays turn out to be the 'taming' of 'Rebellious Susan' and the 'Notorious Mrs. Ebbsmith.' Ibsen's Nora is a rebel with a cause; Galsworthy's Clare is a rebel without one—she leaves her husband because she is simply tried of 'cupboard love' and her prosaic and dull husband. Like Irene she bluntly turns down his offer of reconciliation.

Freda says 'Father brought me up not to whine.'[30] In Clare and Beatrice we have the prototypes of modern sexually liberated women. They turn the tables on their husbands: desertion is no longer a male privilege; weak and prosaic husbands are deserted by their wives who dare to live with their paramours. While *The Fugitive* ends as a tragedy because Clare could not find a suitable match, in *A Bit o' Love* Beatrice obtains divorce from her saintly but ineffectual husband to start a new life with her lover Dr. Desart. It is a refutation of Jones' premise '... poor women cannot retaliate'[31] and Jones' confession in the epistle dedicatory: '... as women cannot retaliate openly, they may retaliate secretly—and *lie.*'[32] New Women in Galsworthy have demonstrated that they too can fight back openly and succeed. Questions may be asked about the justification of Clare's self-annihilation in the last Act. Her tragic death may appear as inconsistent, and sentimental as the death of Mrs. Tanqueray. Galsworthy explained his point of view in his letter to Edward Garnett: 'Women always *seem* to have someone to go to till it comes to the point and then—they simply haven't, especially in that class where appearance have still terrific value. Women, who don't mind planting themselves on others to the inconvenience of and even harm of those others, *have* always someone to go to. But there's the rub, and some women are built so that they can't do that same.'[33]

Galsworthy is a naturalist if we mean by naturalism a portrayal of everyday life with fidelity—as opposed to idealization and rendering of things beautiful when they are not, and presentation of the supernatural or transcendental. Like Ibsen, Shaw and Granville Barker, Galsworthy gave us a faithful representation of Edwardian society. Yet he believed that a realist could be idealistic, poetic, fantastic or impressionistic—almost anything but romantic. Romance has hardly any place in his plays. His characters fall in love under the pressure of circumstances. Love is a matter of life and death to them.

A noteworthy feature of Galsworthy's later plays is that most of his male protagonists are weak and medicore in contrast with his resilient and resourceful female protagonists. We have young maids like Faith and Freda who surpass their lovers in courage and determination to own responsibility. Married women like Clare Dedmond, Mrs. Builders and Beatrice defy social censure to follow the voice of their conscience. They are also more articulate than their male counterparts. Shavian women are of course more voluble but they often give the impression of a make-believe world—characters manipulated to express the view of their creator. With fewer words, often with mute scenes, Galsworthy achieves greater dramatic effect.

If Galsworthy's artistic technique was as much subjected to criticism as the blatant method of Shaw, both would expose their limitations. Physiologically and psychologically, male authors can explore women's problems from the outside only—even their best efforts cannot transcend sympathy or condescension. But what is needed is empathy—an identification with others' feelings from inside. In *Joy* Galsworthy comes closer to a woman's point of view. In *Windows* he deals with a young woman's problem which is finally resolved by her intuition. The concept of the 'New Woman' may be criticised as a mere projection of male fantasy. But she cannot be a fantasy which is the result of wishful thinking and often made the staple food of commercial theatre to entice the starved audience and ensure box-office success. The deficiency of Galsworthy's women is compensated by their credibility. Their lack of spiritual convictions and the spirit of social service is offset by their consistent struggle for changing the lop-sided power structure between the sexes.

Male playwrights by and large cannot truly represent women's perception or their point of view. In their over enthusiasm they often create larger-than-life characters. Shaw is a case in point. His superwomen like Lina, Lesbia, Vivie Warren and Lady Cicely are closer to fantasies, if we mean by fantasy pleasing mental images, usually serving to fulfill a need not gratified in real life. But the women of Granville Barker cannot be dismissed easily as either wish-fulfilment or a projection of archetypes embedded in the collective unconscious of the human race. With the progress in the women's suffragist movement and increasing exposure to uniform education, women began to prove their worth. Real life influenced dramatic literature no less than literature influenced real life. To the highly sensitive mind and sophisticated taste of Virginia

Woolf, 'It is fatal to be a man or woman, pure and simple; one must be woman-manly or man-womanly.'[34] She further expostulates: 'The fact is that neither Mr. Galsworthy nor Mr. Kipling has a spark of the woman in him. Thus, all their qualities seem to a woman, if one may generalize, crude and immature. They lack suggestive power.'[35] Galsworthy's insight into the human problem is evident in *Strife*. The play is not so much about Capital and Labour as it is about the evils of extremism or fanaticism. The diehard strike leader cares little about his sick and starving wife. The two headstrong men fight till they lose their position. The strike takes its toll of the poor worker's wife. Women are shown as the worst sufferers. At the time of prosperity they are unable to control their men from drinking and gambling; in poverty they go without food and medical care. In the Board Meeting of the company the undeserved suffering of women is discussed at length but nothing is done to mitigate it. The strike is withdrawn with no gain for either side: 'A woman dead; and the two best men both broken.'[36] Another victim of the male power game is Chloe in *The Skin Game*. Caught up in a battle between the aristocratic Hillcrist and the nouveau riche Hornblower over the purchase of a property, she is blackmailed for her past occupation as an agent hired for proving misconduct in divorce cases. To save her reputation she is compelled to bribe the agent with all her savings, pearls, even her body, but without success. As a woman her doom is inevitable and inescapable. Following her exposure by the agent and desertion by her husband, she throws herself into a gravel pit. Women, Galsworthy poignantly shows, pay the price of male power politics with their lives.

In sharp contrast with the victimized women of the early plays, Galsworthy created another breed of women like Mrs. Gwyn, Ann, Freda and Clare who dare to defy Victorian conventions. The typical Victorian mother's role is shunned by Mrs. Gwyn in *Joy*. As a separated wife and mother she refuses to give up her lover Maurice Lever even when her teen-aged daughter Joy objects to such relationship in jealousy. She shows strong hatred for her mother's lover and is possessive about her mother. As an only child raised by a single parent, she shows symptoms of compulsive-obsessive behaviour towards her mother and her lover. Perturbed as she is by her neurotic outbursts, she never forgets her duty to self and asserts her autonomy: 'What I am is my affair—not yours—do you understand?' She refuses to conform to the image of a sacrificing mother and asserts her independence: '... Am I to live all my life like a dead woman because you are ashamed? Am I to live like the dead because you're a child that knows nothing of life?'[37]

With an outright rejection of the ideal of self-denial Mrs. Gwyn turns down her immature daughter's offer to 'be everything' to her if she gives up Lever. With her pragmatic sense and enlightened self-interest, she is Galsworthy's first New Woman in quest of a fuller life. The influence of Turgenev and Maupassant and his commitment to Naturalism prompted Galsworthy to draw men and women of average ability; hence his heroines are not intellectual or moral stalwarts like Shaw's and Granville Barker's. This low-key characterization appears to be more consistent with his literary ambition.

The Eldest Son has the recurrent theme of the complacency and the indifference of the upper-middle class to the suffering of the working class. The heroine Freda is a weak and dependent lady's maid in the family of baronet Sir William Cheshire. She becomes pregnant as a result of her intimacy with Sir William's son Bill which leads to the crisis when Lady Chesire discovers the secret affair. Far from denying his relationship, Bill acknowledges his engagement to Freda in public. Unmoved by lady Cheshire's persuasion to give up Bill, she asserts herself by pointing out the similarity of her case with Rose Taylor's liasion with the underkeeper who has been threatened with dismissal. Bill is blamed for his decision to stick to this unequal marriage which will ruin their social status and invite ridicule from the socialists and the Radicals. Sir Cheshire is evidently guilty of double standards when he threatens to disinherit Bill for his decision. The family is saved from disgrace when Freda's father rejects this 'charity marriage' and leaves the service with triumphant self-esteem and dignity.

Galsworthy, the most precise and systematic of realists, brings out the fact of women's oppression and their struggle, often futile, to end it. Freda gives up Bill to avoid a forced and loveless marriage but decides to give birth to the child without any financial aid from the Cheshire family. This play has another assertive and articulate woman named Dot who shoots and rides with great energy and prefers to be 'a private in German regiment than a woman'[38] and is sharply critical when women are kept in blinkers and marriage binds people who no longer love each other. Freda and Dot prove that the New Woman is classless. Though Galsworthy wrote *The Eldest Son* in April and May of 1909 and sent it to Frohmann for performance, it was deferred by James Berrie till Granville Barker decided to produce it in 1912. The play had a fair success, according to Ada Galsworthy's record, with the usual commercial failure.

The Fugitive explores the fate of an emancipated woman in Edwardian society that values loyalty and devotion. Clare Dedmond begins where Ibsen's Nora ended. Her conscience does not permit her to live with George, a well-born and wealthy husband though a trifling dull. Galsworthy shows how she is haunted by her husband's family which is rich and powerful. Her social displacement, an attempt at financial independence, an unsuccessful love-affair with a bohemian artist and the final blind date with a young a man before suicide focus on the inequality between the sexes, not as a result of biological differences but because of the cultural construct. To the Edwardain audience Clare seemed a rebel without a cause. Her husband discovers her departure just before the arrival of his parents. The outraged family tries to patch up the broken marriage without success. Tired of what she called 'cupboard love' Clare dares to lead an independent life. Her maverik friend Malaise encourages her to break out of 'the prison' and spread her wings but cannot help her make a living. She rebuffs all appeals from George Dedmond's family to be reconciled. Disillusioned with her marriage which she considers nothing but 'a lie, a farce' she turns to Malaise for love and stays with him. She learns type-writing for him but she is dismayed when he does not return her love. Once again she leaves her man in despair as living together without the bond of love troubles her conscience. Moreover, Malaise is forced to withdraw his support when the Dedmonds use their clout to stop his income. Having no alternative Clare is compelled to adopt the world's oldest profession. In utter frustration and further wounded by an uncharitable remark by men, she consumes poison to end her life—a tragic waste of a spirited woman who would not conform to male demands. Alec Frechet wrote in *John Galsworthy: A Reassessment*: 'Galsworthy was, as it were, the litmus paper that was to reveal the great contemporary conflicts of society.'[39] Here he shows the heavy price women have to pay to attain their liberation.

In February 1913 Galsworthy visited Chevrillons and revised *The Fugitive*. He explained to the Frenchman the curious idealism which prevented Clare from accepting any assistance from her husband to whom she could not offer her body and soul. She undergoes hardship for a clean conscience. Galsworthy thought that woman's position in France was distinctly lower than in England. The sentimental laxity in marriage of the French male is more a matter of convenience than emancipation of women from male desire or design. Gerald Du Maurier, a well known actor—manager at Wyndham's Theatre wanted to produce the play but was depressed to read it. He failed to understand it, disliked the characters and disapproved of the suicide. He thought it to be a tragedy of 'fey' woman. Galsworthy explained to him that the play is about the tragedy of ladyhood. A woman bred and brought up in a cultured environment fares reasonably well but is neither hardy nor coarse-fibred enough for the cross winds of life. Such women are too fine to stoop really low and not fine enough to make good in spite of everything. It is quite a depressing subject—truth sometimes is. However, Galsworthy admitted that Du Maurier's dislike is likely to be shared by most people.[40] An unknown correspondent associated Clare with Irene as both characters show an abhorrence for sexual relationship with men they dislike. However, H.W. Nevinson considered the play hardly modern and remarked that real women in similar situations escaped such a tragic fate. A New Woman like Clare may not succeed in dismantling male hegemony but she at least strikes at the root of feminine virtues like constancy and self-abnegation and asserts her autonomy. In the hands of a bolder dramatist, her death would not have been inevitable.

More aggressive is Mrs. Beatrice Strangway who elopes with her former lover Dr. Desart and returns only to seek release from her saintly but effeminate husband. *A Family Man* portrays the declining power of a patriarch whose tyranny forces his wife and daughters to leave. His alienated elder daughter elopes with an artist without marrying him. The younger daughter follows suit. Next to go is Mrs. Builder who is infected with a yearning for liberty. Even the French maid to whom he turns for love leaves him in disgust. At the end of the play he finds himself in splendid isolation and finally is imprisoned for striking his own child and assaulting a constable. Though not a drama of high merit *A Family Man* records the transformation that was taking place in regard to women's status in society. An enterprising role is played by Ann in *The Pigeons*. As a prudent daughter she undertakes the tough task of extricating her philanthropist father from the parasites who fleece him for their selfish end. Only Mrs. March in *Windows* comes close to an intellectual woman who mocks her psychological novelist husband for his inability to penetrate the human psyche. Her epiphany in the Final Act saves the family from disintegration.

On the whole Galsworthy's plays focus on the problems of the average man and woman which often originate from a lack of sympathy and imaginative understanding of human nature. This women characters range from the victims of social and legal discrimination in *The Silver Box*, *Strife* and *Justice* to the discontented and defiant wives in *The Fugitive* and *A Bit o' Love,* who desert their husbands without any compunction. His women are more evolutionary than revolutionary. Their personalities keep growing from passive victims to assertive young maids. As a result of induction of the New Woman the conventional conflict between the upper and the lower classes is changed to the conflict between the sexes—a fact overlooked in criticism. From the stereotype sufferer to bold dissenter is a long evolutionary journey. The battle waged by Mrs. Gwyn, Clare and Freda against the patriarchal tradition is an arduous one; and victory is not always within reach. But they keep the torch burning.

The new drama that emerged in 1890s became a living social force. The New Women in the plays of Shaw, Granville Barker and Galsworthy represent a new moral outlook and bring about a new power equation. She is the prototype of the modern heroine whose equality and independence is taken for granted.

NOTES AND REFERENCES

1. *English Drama (1900-1930)* (London, Cambridge University, 1973), p. 400.
2. *Galsworthy: Ten Best Plays* (London, Duckworth, 1976), p. 6.
3. *Henry Arthur Jones: Plays* (London, Cambridge University, 1982), p. 160.
4. *Year's Work in English Studies* Vol-70 (1989), p. 497.
5. Toby Cole ed., *Playwrights on Playwriting* (N. York, Hill & Wang, 1961), p. 45.
6. *Ibid.*, p. 46.
7. *Ibid.*
8. *Ibid.*
9. Margaret Morris, *My Galsworthy Story*, (London, Peter Owen, 1967) p. 69.
10. *Ibid.*, pp. 131-132.
11. John Galsworthy, *The Forsyte Saga* (London, W. Heinemann, 1948) p. 681.
12. *Ibid.*, p. viii.
13. *Ibid.*, p. 413.
14. *Ibid.*, (1936 ed.) 652.
15. *Ibid.*, p. 658.
16. *Ibid.*, p. xii.

17. D.H. Lawrence, *Selected Essays* (Harmondsworth, Penguin, 1950) pp. 220-21.
18. *Ibid.*, p. 223.
19. *Ibid.*, p. 224.
20. *Ibid.*, p. 225.
21. *Ibid.*, p. 227.
22. *Playwrights on Playwrighting*, p. 151.
23. Henry Arthur Jones, *Plays* (London, Cambridge University, 1982), p. 107.
24. Simon Trussler, *Cambridge Illustrated History of British Theatre* (London, Cambridge University, 1974), p. 268.
25. *Galsworthy: Ten Best Plays*, pp. 63-64.
26. *John Galsworthy: Five Plays* (London, Methuen, 1984), p. 144.
27. *Ibid.*
28. *Ibid.*, p. 123.
29. *Playwrights on Playwriting*, p. 45.
30. *Galsworthy: Five Plays*, p. 133.
31. H.A. Jones: *Plays*, p. 160.
32. *Ibid.*, p. 107.
33. Edward Garnell, ed., *Letters from Galsworthy (1900-1932)* (Jonathan Cape, N.York, 1934), p. 212.
34. Virginia Woolf, *A Room of One's Own and Three Guineas* (London, Chatto & Windus, 1984), p. 24.
35. *Ibid.*, p. 95.
36. *Galsworthy: Ten Best Plays*, p. 73.
37. *Ibid.*, p. 58.
38. *John Galsworthy: Five Plays* (London, Methuen, 1984), p. 144.
39. Denis Mahefey, trans., *John Galsworthy: A Reassessment*, (London, Macmillan, 1982), p. vii.
40. Jack J. Gindin, *John Galsworthy's Life and Art*, (London, Macmillan, 1987), p. 322.

CONCLUSION

6

The feminist movement of the nineteenth century was able to draw attention of the public to women as a group having special interests and aspirations. But the limitations were also obvious. Most women's lives were untouched by the movement for emancipation. Their longing for breaking the traditional cage of 'the Woman's sphere' was not followed by their participation in the feminist campaigns. Women's achievements were more individual than of the gender. Bertha Von Suttner was awarded the Nobel prize for Peace in 1905. Marie Curie won two Nobel prizes for science in 1903 and 1911. In 1895 the prominent women who made it to the Who's Who came largely under the heading 'Reformers, Philanthropists etc.' The number of intellectual women was not negligible: there were forty-eight authors and forty-two stage personalities. The number of female doctors rose from 20 in 1881 to 212 in 1901 and 447 in 1911. Much more problematic was the question of sexual liberation. Admired by Fourier and Bebel, it was practised only by a few bohemians and propangandists. Moreover, the question of sexual freedom was linked up with the right and privilege of motherhood. But all the important problems found their place in the drama.

The Woman Question was raised by Pinero and Jones in a passive and perfunctory manner but was effectively put on the stage by Shaw, Granville Barker and Galsworthy. The New Women inducted by these playwrights are remarkable for their intelligence, dynamism and pragmatic outlook. They show awareness of their bondage as women and struggle to shake off their shackles. Some of them, like Grace and Lesbia, turn down offers of comfortable home and hearth, some like Amy resort to violent revenge and some others like Mrs. Gwyn and

Beatrice dismantle the image of the sacrificing mother and the passive wife.

Though the New Woman of the dramatic revival cannot be equated with the feminist of the 1960s and seventies, she may reasonably claim to be her precursor. Caryl Churchill warned us about mixing up of ostensible drama about women and feminist drama. Michelene Wandor, another feminist playwright and critic, points out the fact that most plays embody a male outlook and the protagonists are invariably male. Women appear either as adjuncts to male characters or are seen as ciphers. Women have rarely been the subjects of drama in their own right or in relations with men.[1] But Megan Terry, the mother of American feminist theatre, has a broader definition: '.... anything that gives women confidence, shows themselves to themselves, helps them to analyse whether it's a positive or negative image ...'[2] may pass as feminist drama. The range of the New Woman in the plays of Shaw, Granville Barker and Galsworthy is as wide as the manifold feminisms of our time. While Granville Barker and Galsworthy were content to depict the struggle and status of the average woman in a more or less naturalistic manner, Shaw went a step further by modelling his new heroines on the extra-ordinary women of his time like Annie Besant, Ellen Terry and Beatrice Webb.

As the feminist drama of the 1980s has its roots in the political and aesthetic disruption of the 1960s, the new drama has a historical underpinning of the 1890s in the suffragist movement of the last decade of the nineteenth century. Since the early sixties roughly 300 plays by women playwrights have been published in the U.K. and the U.S.A. They are born of a feminist consciousness and illuminate women's roles and explore their relationship with men in society. At least another 100 feminist plays have been produced but remain unpublished. Some of the techniques of the feminist theatre were curiously anticipated. Shaw is a master in the art of gender role-reversal. In *Man and Superman* and *Candida* he stunned the audience with one of his heroines chasing her lover and another, a housewife, asserting her right to choose between her husband and her lover. If success, personal autonomy, affirmation of women's strength and sexual freedom are the criteria of modern feminist theatre, the plays under review in the present dissertation have more than a fair share of these qualities.

The emergence of the New Woman brought a new power equation in the drama: the role of the protagonist ceased to be a male monopoly. Their understanding of sexual politics leads them to reject the stereotyped image of the dutiful daughter and submissive wife. The romantic heroines of the commercial theatre are replaced by a tough breed of educated women who are more or less androgynous. Women like Grace, Lina, Lesbia, Lady Cicely and Mrs. Gwyn exist by their own right. Some plays like *Joy*, *Windows* and *Getting Married* explore the problems of love and sexuality from the feminine perspective. The achievements of the New Woman seem no longer remarkable after the lapse of a century: they have become permanent features of modern drama. Deconstruction of the female archetype is as much an integral part of the playwrights' art as is the negation of their sexual role. It is not easy to assess the impact of the New Woman on the lives of real women; but I have endeavoured to show her impact on the theatre and the evolution of the modern heroine. By 1983 the number of women playwrights rose to about 110 out of 547. There was hardly any woman playwright a century ago. A numerical ratio of male and female characters is two and half to one, according to Britain's leading drama publishers. Michelen Wandor, who was involved with the Women's Liberation movement in 1969-70, notes with disappointment that women are clustered at the base of the hierarchical pyramid in terms of income, artistic and administrative power; very few women reach the top and actresses earn much less than actors.[3]

Women's right to sexual freedom is the subject of Pam Gem's *Piaf*, Caryl Churchill's masterpiece *Top Girls*, and Nell Dunn's *Steaming*. Shaw's *The Philanderer* and Galsworthy's *A Bit o' Love* explored the same theme with equal frankness a century ago. These plays were far ahead of their time and it was a long time before they were accepted by the audience. John Builder expressed it very candidly in *A Family Man*: 'Men do not like the new spirit in women—they may say they do, but they don't.'[4] The New Women were thus engaged in a twofold battle: on the one hand they challenged the codes and conventions of a patriarchal society, on the other they had to overcome their own passivity which is summed up in Caryl Churchill's *Fen*—the sun and the moon urge women to 'turn back' but they refuse to turn back for anyone. This slightly pessimistic comment suggests a Hardyesque philosophy which presupposes men and women to be victims of a power beyond human control. Despite her feminist sensibility, Churchill is not anti-men. The successful feminist characters of her plays pay the price of their liberation by way of loneliness and childlessness.

The New Woman is a bridge between the Victorian stereotype and the overt feminist of the nineteen eighties. The plays with the New Woman as the central character are less known and had lesser box office success for the obvious reason that Victorian and Edwardian women could not identify themselves with the stage figures and men frowned at their liberation. In her evolutionary journey of a hundred years the feminist heroines have picked up a lot of four-letter words which now sprinkle their speeches. The New Women of Shaw, Galsworthy and Granville Barker have been instrumental in changing the character and status of the heroine. The duel of the sexes is polemical in Shaw. In Galsworthy it is due to the conflicting values of the classes. In Barker the personality clashes are subdued in the interest of moral and social uplift.

A distinguishing feature of the New Woman was her new morality which prompted her to reject much of the obsolescent conventions. But this new morality is never unethical. In comparison the heroines of the modern feminist theatre is best described as amoral. In Pam Gems' *Dusa, Fish, Stas and Vi* Dusa displays 'particular vulnerability of the breeding bitch.'[5] Violet is introduced as '... the remnant of hippie culture—bits of punk.' Stas is a physiotherapist who tries part-time prostitution to finance her study of marine biology. Fish who asserts: 'The right to take decisions about our own lives is one we have to fight for.'[6] But she makes the dubious decision of taking her own life in frustration. In her suicide note she raises the million dollar question: 'My loves, what are we to do? We won't do as they want any more, and they hate it. What are we to do?'[7] Many a feminist would disapprove of such emotional as well as psychological dependence on men. To a successful executive like Marlene in *Top Girls* women's transformation is permanent and irreversible. Men are 'waiting for me to turn into the little woman.'[8] As a career woman she can dispense with men easily like Vivie Warren for the sake of autonomy.

The transformation of 'the little woman' into a feminist is a long evolutionary process. A great turning point in real life as well as in dramatic literature was the emergence of the New Woman. In speech and action she is surprisingly modern and anticipates much of the feminist theatre of modern era. She played a crucial role in introducing sexual politics in the theatre. My efforts have been directed to the task of assessing her contribution to modern drama. In the theatre, the New Woman transformed the conventional feminine role in the same way as the suffragists did for the common woman's lot in general.

NOTES AND REFERENCES

1. Michelene Wandor, *Drama Today* (Longman, London, 1993) p. 17.
2. Helen Keysaar, *Feminist Theatre* (Macmillan, London, 1986) p. 53.
3. M. Wandor, *Drama Today* (Longman, London, 1993) pp. 15-16.
4. John Galsworthy, *A Family Man* (Duckworth, London, 1922) pp. 21-22.
5. Pam Gems, *Dusa, Fish, Stas and Vi* (Samuel French, London, 1977) p. 5.
6. *Ibid.*, p. 17.
7. *Ibid.*
8. Caryl Churchill, *Top Girls* (Methuen, London, 1984).

BIBLIOGRAPHY

Alardyce Nicoll, *A History of English Drama*, Vol-V Cambridge, Cam. Un., 1955.

Allen, W. Dennis, *Sexuality in Victorian Fiction*, Norman, Oklahama Un. Press, 1993.

Altick, D. Richard, *The Art of Literary Research*, N. York, W.W. Norton & Co, 1981.

Ashley, Maurice, *The People of England: A short social and Economic History*, London, Weidenfeld & Nicholeson, 1982.

American Studies Research Centre, *The MLA Style Sheet*, Hyderabad, ed. 1970.

Barker, Dudley, *The Man of Principle*, London, Heinenamann, 1963.

Barker, Harley Granville, *The Madras House*, London, Methuen, 1977.

Barker, H. Granville, *The Collected Plays*, London, Sidwick & Jackson, 1967.

Barker, H. Granville, *Plays: one*, Methuen, London, 1993.

Barry, Peter, *Beginning Theory: An Introduction to Literary and cultural Theory* Manchester, Manchester Un. Press., 1995.

Bentley, Eric, *Playwright As Thinker: A study of Drama in Modern Times*, New York, Reynal & Hitchock, 1946.

Bentley, Eric, *Bernard Shàw*, London, Robert Hale Ltd., 1950.

Bentley, Eric, *Theatre of War*, New York, Eyre Methuen, 1972.

Bentley, Eric, *The Life of the Drama*, London, Methuen, 1965.

Bernauer, James, ed., *The Final Foucault*, Cambridge, M.I.T. Press, 1987.

Brad brool, M.C., *Women and Literature, 1779-1982*, vol-2, Sussex, Harvester Press, 1982.

Bronowski, J., *The Ascent of Man*, London, BBC, 1990.

Caudwell, Christopher, *Studies in a Dying Culture*, London, M.R., 1971.

Churchill, Caryl, *Top Girls*, London, Methuen, 1984.

Clarke, Ian, *Edwardian Drama*, London, Faber & Faber, 1989.

Coats, R.H., *John Galsworthy As a Dramatic Artist*, London, Duckworth, 1976.

Coyle, Martin, Ed., *Encyclopedia of Literature and Criticism*, London, Routledge, 1990.

Crowley, Heten and Himmelweit, Susan, ed., *Knowing Women: Feminism and Knowledge*, Cambridge, Polity Press, 1992.

Daiches, David, *Critical Approaches to Literature*, Essex, Longman, 1981.

Das, Sisir Kumar, *An Introduction to Research*, Calcutta, A. Mukherjee & Co., 1986.

Delenze, Gilles, *Foucault*, London, Athlone Press, 1988.

Digby, Anne, and Feinstein, ed., *New Directions in Economic and Social History*, London, Macmillan, 1989.

Dobree, Bonamy, *Modern Prose Style*, London, O.U.P., 1964.

Dobree, Bonamy, *The Lamp and the Lute*, London, Frank Cass, 1964.

Downs, Brian W., *Ibsen: Intellectual Back ground*, London, Cambridge, Un., 1946.

Duffin, H.C., *The Quintessence of Bernard Shaw*, London, Allen and Unwin, 1939.

Dukore, F. Bernard, *Bernard Shaw, Playwright*, Columbia Missouri Un. Press, 1973.

Dupont, V., *John Galsworthy: The Dramatic Artist*, Lyon Folcroft Press, 1970.

Dupre, Cathy, *John Galeworthy: A Biography*, London, Collins, 1976.

Dymkowski, Christine, *Harley Granville Barker*, London, Folger Books, 1986.

Eagleton, Mary, ed., *Feminist Literary Criticism*, London, Longman, 1991.

Egan, Michael, Ed., *Ibsen, Critical Heritage*, London, Routiedge & Kegan Paul, 1972.

Ervine, St. John, *Bernard Shaw: His Life, Work and Friends*, London, Constable, 1956.

Estelle, Phillips, & Pugh, D.S. *How to Get PHD*, London, Open Un. 1992.

Evans, Judith, *et al. Feminism and Political Theory*, London, Sage Publication, 1986.

Evans, F.T., ed., *Shaw: The Critical Heritage*, London, Routiedge, 1976.

Evans, Lloyd Gareth, *The Language of Modern Drama*, London, Dent, 1977.

Evans, Mary ed., *The Woman Question*, London, Sage Publication, 1994.

Fabb, Nigel and Durant Alan, *How to Write Essays, Dissertations and Theses in Literary Studies*, London, Longman, 1993.

Ferando, Lloyd, "*New Women" in the Late Victorian Novel*, London, Pennsylvania Un, 1977.

Fjelde, Rolf, trsl., *Complete Major Plays by Ibsen*, New York, Farrar, 1978.

Foucault, Michele, *The History of Sexuality*, vols, I & II, Harmondsworth, 1984.

Frechet, Alec, *John Galsworthy: A Reassessment*, London, Macmillan, 1982.

Friedan, Betty, *Feminine Mystique*, London, Victor Gollancz, 1963.

Gallop, Jane, *Reading Lacan*, Ithaca, Cornell Un., 1985.

Galsworthy, John, *A Bit O'Love,* London, Duckworth, 1915.

Galsworthy, John, *The Forsyte Saga*, London W. Heinmann, 1936 & 1948.

Galsworthy, John, *Five Plays*, London, Methuen, 1984.

Galsworthy, John, *A Family Man,* London, Duckworth, 1922.

Garnett, Edward, ed., *Letters from Galsworthy (1900-1932)*, N. York, Jonathan Cape, 1932.

Gascoigne, Bamber, *Twentieth Century Drama*, London, HUtchinson Un. Library, 1967.

Gems, Pam, *Dusa, Fish, Stas and Vi*, London, Samuel French, 1977.

Gibbs, A.M., *The Art and Mind of Shaw*, Dublin, Macmillan, 1983.

Gibbs, A.M., Ed., *Shaw: Interviews and Recollections*, London, Macmillan, 1990.

Gillette, Eric, *Galsworthy: Ten Best Plays*, London, Duckworth, 1976.

Gillian, Kersley, *Darling Madam*, London, Virago, 1983.

Gindin, James Jack, *John Galsworthy's Life and Art*, London, Macmiilan, 1987.

Gray, John, *Men are from Mars, Women are from Venus*, New Delhi, Harper Collins, India, 1993.

Greer, Germaine, *The Female Eunuch*, London, Paladin, 1970.

Griffth, A. Philips, *Philosophy and Literature*, London, Camb. Un., 1984.

Hill, Maureen, *Women in the 20th Century*, London, Chapmans, 1991.

Hobsbawn, E.J., *The Age of Empire*, London, Weidenfeld and Nicholson, 1987.

Holroyd Michael, *Bernard Shaw*, Vols.1-4, London, Chatto & Windus, 1988.

Holroyd, Michael, *The Genius of Shaw: A Symposium*, London Hodder & Stroughton, 1979.

Horney, Karen, *Feminine Psychology*, London, Routledge & K. Paul, 1967.

Huang, Jolin, *Shaw and Galsworthy*, Norwood, pa., 1979.

Innes, Christopher, *Modern British Drama, 1890-1990*, Cambridge, Cambridge Un., 1992.

Jackson, Russell, Ed., *Plays by Henry Arthur Jones*, London, Cambridge Un., 1982.

Jefferson, Ann and Robey Daird, ed., *Modern Literary Theory*, B.T. Batsford, London, 1986.

Jenkins, Anthony, *The Making of Victorian Drama*, Cambridge, Cambridge Un., 1991.

Johnson, Joshephine, *Florence Farr*, Bucks, Colin Smythe, 1975.

Kennedy, Dennis, Ed., *Granville Barker: Plays*, London, Cambridge Un., 1987.

Kettle, Arnold, *Literature and Liberation*, Manchester, Manchester Un. Press, 1988.

Laurence, Dan H., and Leary Daniel, J., Eds., *Bernard Shaw: The Complete Prefaces*, Vol. I, London, Allen Lane, 1993.

Laurence, Dan, H., ed., *Bernard Shaw: Collected Letters*, 3 Vols, London, Max Reinhardt, 1985.

Laurence, Dan H., ed., *Bernard Shaw: Platform and Pulpit*, London, Rupert Hart Davis, 1962.

Laurence, D. H., *Selected Literary Criticism*, Melbourne, William Heinemann, 1955.

Lawrence, D.H., *Selected Essays*, Harmondsworth, Penguin, 1950.

Lee, Jennette, *The Ibsen Secret*, New York, G.P. Putnam's Sons, 1907.

Lemart, C. Charles, and Gillan Garth, *Michel Foucault*, New York Columbia Un., 1982.

Longford, Elizabeth, *Eminent Victorian Women*, London, Weitenfield & Nicholson, 1981.

Lorichs, Sonja, *The Unwomanly Woman in Bernard Shaw's Drama*, Stockholm, Uppasala Un. 1973.

Lovell, Terry, ed., *British Feminist Thought*, Oxford, Basil Blackwell, 1990.

Lucas, F.L., *The Drama of Ibsen and Strindberg*, London, Cassell. 1962.

Martin, Howard, *Britain Since 1800: Towards the Welfare State*, London, Macmillan, 1988.

Martin, Meisel, *Shaw and the 19th Century Theatre*, New Jersy, Princeton Un. Press, 1963.

Marurick, Arthur, *Britain in our Century*, London, Thames & Hudson, 1984.

May, M. Keith, *Ibsen and Shaw*, London, Macmillan, 1985.

Mcdonald, Jan, *The New Drama: 1900-1914*, London, Macmillan, 1986.

Mcarthy, Desmond, *Shaw*, London, Mac Gibbon & Kee 1951.

Mehra, Manmohan *Harley Granville Barker*, Calcutta, Naya Prakash, 1981.

Meyer, Michael, *Henrik Ibsen: The Making of a Dramatist*, London, Rupert Hart-Davis, 1967.

Mill, John Stuart, *The Subjection of Women*, M.I.T. Press, Cambridge, 1970.

Millet, Kate, *Sexual Politics*, London, Rupert Hart-Davis, 1971.

Mitchell, Juliet, *Psychoanalysis and Feminism*, London, Allen Lane, 1974.

Mitchell, Juliet, and Oakley, Ann, *What is Feminism*? Oxford, Basil Black Well, 1986.

Morgan, M. Margery, *The Shavian Playground*, London, Methuen, 1972.

Morgan, M. Margery, *A Drama of Political Man*, London, Sidwick & Jackson, 1961.

Morris, Margaret, *My Galsworthy Story*, London, Petter Owen, 1967.

Morris, Pam, *Literature and Feminism*, Oxford, Blackwell, 1993.

Morrison, Harry, *The Socialism of Bernard Shaw*, Jefferson Mac Farland & Co.,

Okleys, Judith, *Simone de Beauvoir*, London, Virago, 1968.

Parker, W.R., *The MLA style Sheet*, Hyderabad, American studies Research Centre, 1970.

Pearson, Hesketh, *Bernard Shaw:* His Life and Personality, London, Methuen, 1961.

Pickering, Kenneth, *How to Study Modern Drama*, London, Macmillan, 1988.

Pitt, Angela, *Shakespeare's Women*. London, David and Charles, 1981.

Purdom, B.C., *Bernard Shaw's Letters to G. Barker*, London, Phoenix House, 1956.

Ragland-Sullivan, *Jacques Lacan and the Philosophy of Psychoanalysis*, London, Croom Helm, 1986.

Robyn, R. Warhol, and Diane Price Herndl, *Feminisms*, New Burnswick Rutger University, 1991.

Rossi, S. Alice, ed., *The Feminist Papers*, New York, Columbia, 1973.

Routh & Woolff, *The Sociology of Literature: Theortical Approaches*, Keele, University of Keele, 1977.

Rowbotham, Sheila, *Women in Movement*, New York, Routeledge, 1992.

Rowbothan, Sheila, *Women, Resistance and Revolution*, London, Penguin, 1972.

Rowell, George, ed., *A.W. Pinero: Plays*, London, Cambridge Un., 1986.

Russell, Jackson. ed., *Arthur Henry Jones: Plays*, London, Cambridge Un., 1982.

Salenius, W. Elmer, *Harley Granville Barker*, Boston, Twayne Publishers, 1982.

Salmon, Eric, *Granville Barlker: A Secret Life*, London, Heinemann, 1983.

Schalit, Leon, *John Galsworthy: A Survey*, London, William Heinmann, 1929.

Selden, Raman, *A Reader's Guide to Contemporary Literary Theory*, Sussex, Harvester Press, 1985.

Sen, Amartya, *Ethics and Economics*, Oxford, Basil Blackwell, 1987.

Shaw, G. Bernard, *Everybody's Political What's What*, London, Constable, 1945.

Shaw, G. Bernard, *Immaturity*, London, Constable, 1930.

Shaw, G. Bernard, *The Complete Prefaces of Bernard Shaw*, London, Paul Hamlyn, 1965.

Shaw, G. Bernard, *The Irrational Knot*, London, Archibald Anderson, 1905.

Shaw, G. Bernard, *The Complete Plays of Bernard Shaw*, London, Paul Hamlyn, 1965.

Shaw, G.B., *The Quintessence of Ibsenism*, London, Constable & Co. 1913.

Thatcher, Margaret, *The Downing Street Years*, London, Harper Collins, 1993.

Todd, Janet, *Feminist Literary History*, Cambridge, Polity Press, 1988.

Showalter, Elaine, *The New Feminist Criticism*, London, Virago Press, 1986.

Trussler, Simon, *Cambridge Illustrated History of British Theatre*, Cambridge, Cambridge Un. Press, 1994.

Valency, Maurice, *The Flower and the Castle*, New York, Octagon, 1975.

Walder, Dennis, Ed., *Literature in the Modern World*, London, O.U.P., 1990.

Wandor, Michelene, *Drama Today*, London, Longman, 1993.

Wandor, Michelene, *Look Back in Gender*, London, Methuen, 1987.

Waston, Barbara Bellow, *A Shavian Guide to Intelligent Woman*, London, Chatto & Windus, 1964.

Watson, George, *Writing a Thesis*, London, Longman, 1987.

Weintraub, Rodelle, ed., *Fabian Feminist: Bernard Shaw and Women,* University Park Press, Sylvania Un., 1977.

Weintraub, Stanley (ed) *Bernard Shaw: The Diaries 1885-1897*, I & II, University Park, Pennsylvania Un., 1986.

Wellek, Rene, and Warren, Austin, *Theory of Literature*, Harmondsworth, Penguin, 1963.

Wheleham, Imelda, *Modern Feminist Thought*, Edinburgh, Edinburgh Un., 1995.

Whitman, F. Robert, *Shaw and the Play of Ideas*, London, Cornell University Press, 1977.

Willson, Colin, *Bernard Shaw: A Reassessment*, London, Macmillan, 1981.

Wilkes, John, *United Kingdom: A social History of Modern Britain*, Cambridge, Cambridge Un. 1986.

Williams, Raymond, *Drama: Ibsen to Brecht*, London, Chatto & Windus, 1968.

Wilson, Edmund, *The Triple Thinkers*, London, John Lehmann, 1952.

Wollstonecraft, Mary, *A Vindication of the Rights of Woman*, Harmondsworth, Penguin, 1978.

Woolf, Virginia, *A Room of one's own and Three Guineas*, London, Chatto & Windus, 1984.